W9-DCX-590

RIPKEN

No. 8

FROM ABERDEEN TO COOPERSTOWN,
A CELEBRATION OF A HOMETOWN HERO

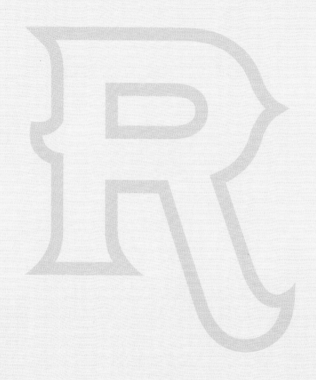

Ripken: From Aberdeen to Cooperstown, A Celebration of A Hometown Hero

is a *PressBox* publication. Copyright © 2007 by Word Smith Media Ventures, LLC. All Rights Reserved. No part of this publication may be reproduced or transmitted in any form without the written consent of the publisher.

Published in the United States of America
by Word Smith Media Ventures, LLC
3600 Clipper Mill Road, Suite 155
Baltimore, MD 21211

ISBN 0-9791975-0-3

PHOTOGRAPHY: Jerry and Scott Wachter/RipkenBOOK.com: Cover, 5, 6, 11, 16, 18, 22, 24, 27, 30, 35, 37, 45, 55, 57, 60, 63, 64. Mitch Stringer/PressBox: 50, 51.

ACKNOWLEDGEMENTS: Cover design and art direction by Brad Meerholz. Graphic design and layout by Jennifer Perkins-Franz. Special projects editor, Jennifer Nelson.

SPECIAL THANKS: Stan Charles, Larry Harris, Kevin Heitz, John Coulson, Rick Marsalek, Tyler Covahey, Mark Luterman, Jeff Hemelt, Frank Oroszlan, Mallory Rubin, Staci Wolfson, Buzz Battaglia, Marvin Milstein and Jay Strecker.

CONTENTS

N° 8

al Ripken Jr. is going to Cooperstown armed with a resume that includes the most votes ever recorded and the third-highest approval rating of all time, but true to his form all the longtime Oriole cared about was the basics.

"It's a tremendous honor to get such a large percentage of the votes (98.53)," Ripken said shortly after being notified on Jan. 9 that he had been named on 537 of the 545 ballots. "But the words 'Congratulations, welcome to the Hall of Fame,' those were the best."

Although there had been considerable speculation that Ripken might be the first inductee ever to get 100 percent

"The other, from a personal standpoint, came on Sept. 6, 1995 (when he broke Lou Gehrig's record of 2,130 consecutive games), when Bobby Bonilla and Raffy (Rafael Palmeiro) pushed me out to take the lap around the field. That turned something that impacted 50,000 people into a one-on-one experience."

When he goes to Cooperstown for his induction, Ripken will have an advantage over most of those who made the trip before him. He will be one of the very few to have witnessed an induction prior to his own, having made the trip in 2003, when former teammate, mentor and close friend Eddie Murray joined what has been called the world's most exclusive fraternity.

WELCOME TO THE HALL

By | Jim Henneman

of the vote, the legendary home-grown Oriole insisted he never dwelled on the subject. "I didn't think about it a lot," he said. "It's a very subjective thing, I suppose — and I respect everybody's opinion."

Instead, he was more than satisfied to reflect on the honor itself and what it might mean to now be considered a "teammate" of his idol, Brooks Robinson, and the other greats of the game. "It seems a little unreal ... I don't know what that's going to feel like, being a teammate of Brooksie's and the others like him.

"It's magical, almost ghostly in some ways, a moving feeling," Ripken said, when asked to describe his emotion after being notified of his election. "It's a glorious day. There was a certain sense of anticipation, of euphoria, a sense of nervousness, and also relief. There were some butterflies ... I wanted to hear those words 'Congratulations, welcome to the Hall of Fame.'"

In reflecting on his career, Ripken compared the moment to two of the other major highlights of his career. "No. 1 as a player was catching the ball for the final out of the World Series (1983)," he said. "There is a great deal of satisfaction and fulfillment in contributing to a championship.

"It was an emotional roller coaster," Ripken said. "It was very moving, and very, very emotional."

It was a scene that undoubtedly will be duplicated July 29, 2007, when Ripken shares the spotlight with Tony Gwynn — both hometown products who played their entire careers with their hometown team. It somehow seems only appropriate that advance reservations from as far back as three years ago indicate this will be the largest crowd ever to convene for an induction.

"I hope it is," Ripken said, "because to me Cooperstown is a celebration of baseball. Every year the Hall of Fame honors individuals, but really, to me, it's a celebration of the past."

And for the kid from Aberdeen who didn't have to wander far from home to leave his mark, it will be the culmination of a special journey. "It's a continuation and celebration of a dream that I was able to live," he said. "I love what I did ... and to be remembered at all is pretty special."

A plaque in Cooperstown will insure that Cal Ripken Jr. is remembered — because he was "pretty special." □

JIM HENNEMAN IS A VETERAN WRITER WHO HAS SERVED AS PRESIDENT OF THE BASEBALL WRITERS' ASSOCIATION OF AMERICA.

ORIOLES IN THE HALL OF FAME

PLAYERS

LUIS APARICIO, SS
1956-73 (1963-67) – .262, 2,677 hits, 83 HR, 394 2B, 506 SB, 791 RBI

REGGIE JACKSON, OF
1967-87 (1976) – .262, 2,584 hits, 563 HR, 463 2B, 228 SB, 1,701 RBI

GEORGE KELL, 3B
1943-57 (1956-57) – .306, 2,054 hits, 78HR, 385 2B, 51 SB, 870 RBI

EDDIE MURRAY,* 1B
1977-97 (1977-88, 1996) – .287, 3,255 hits, 504 HR, 560 2B, 110 SB, 1,917 RBI

JIM PALMER,* P
1965-84 (1965-84) – 268-152, 2.86 ERA, 2,212 SO

ROBIN ROBERTS, P
1948-66 (1962-65) – 286-245, 3.41 ERA, 2,357 SO

BROOKS ROBINSON,* 3B
1955-77 (1955-77) – .267, 2,848 hits, 268 HR, 482 2B, 1,357 RBI

FRANK ROBINSON,* OF
1956-76 (1966-71) – .294, 2,943 hits, 586 HR, 528 2B, 1812 RBI

HOYT WILHELM, P
1952-72 (1958-62) – 143-122, 2.52 ERA, 1,610 SO

MANAGERS

FRANK ROBINSON – 1975-77, 1981-84, 1988-91, 2002-06 (1988-91) - 1065-1176, .475

EARL WEAVER - 1968-82, 1985-86 (1968-82, 1985-86) - 1480-1060, .583

(Years with the Orioles) * Inducted as an Oriole

HIGHEST VOTE PERCENTAGE FOR HALL OF FAME INDUCTEES

	Name	Year Inducted	% of Votes
1.	TOM SEAVER	1992	98.84%
2.	NOLAN RYAN	1999	98.79%
3.	TY COBB	1936	98.23%
4.	GEORGE BRETT	1999	98.19%
5.	HANK AARON	1982	97.83%
6.	MIKE SCHMIDT	1995	96.52%
7.	JOHNNY BENCH	1989	96.42%
8.	STEVE CARLTON	1994	95.82%
9.	BABE RUTH	1936	95.13%
	HONUS WAGNER	1936	95.13%
11.	WILLIE MAYS	1979	94.68%
12.	CARL YASTRZEMSKI	1989	94.63%
13.	BOB FELLER	1962	93.75%
14.	REGGIE JACKSON	1993	93.62%
15.	TED WILLIAMS	1966	93.38%
16.	STAN MUSIAL	1969	93.24%
17.	ROBERTO CLEMENTE	1973	92.69%
18.	JIM PALMER	1990	92.57%
19.	BROOKS ROBINSON	1983	91.98%
20.	WADE BOGGS	2005	91.86%

FROM NATIONAL BASEBALL HALL OF FAME AND MUSEUM, BASEBALLHALLOFFAME.ORG

It probably skipped the notice of local baseball historians, but the year 2007 represents a special milestone in Orioles history.

It marks the 50th anniversary of the late Cal Ripken Sr.'s professional debut as a catcher for Phoenix, a Class C Orioles farm club. After his unheralded debut, Cal Sr. spent the next 37 years serving the Orioles as a minor league player and manager, scout, roving instructor, big-league coach, and ultimately earned a promotion to manage the parent club in 1987. Cal Sr.'s days as an Oriole ended with his abrupt and controversial firing by then-owner Edward Bennett Williams after the 1988 season was only six games old.

In many respects, Cal Sr. put a bigger stamp on the Baltimore franchise than fiery Earl Weaver in establishing

Two family anecdotes in particular characterize these admirable traits that Cal Jr. later adopted as motivation to maintain the record-breaking consecutive-game streak.

His father's penchant for perseverance became part of Ripken clan folklore. His offspring humorously recall how Cal Sr. patiently waited to ambush a groundhog that had been feasting on the family's patch of cantaloupes and watermelons.

Awakening at dawn, he equipped himself with the morning newspaper, a thermos of coffee, a pack of cigarettes and a shotgun. After two hours, the groundhog finally appeared, making a beeline for a row of newly-grown string beans. It took only one shot from the Orioles' ultimate straight shooter to dispose

THE RIPKEN WAY

By | Alan Goldstein

a how-to manual for teaching minor leaguers The Oriole Way. That formula preached the same fundamentals for executing the hit-and-run, relay plays, rundowns and bunt coverage until it became standard procedure for players from Class D to the major league team.

As Cal Sr. often lectured, "Do two million little things right and the big things take care of themselves."

But for all his years of preparing and mentoring minor leaguers and future Orioles, Cal Sr. will always be best remembered for the major influence he had on the career of his son, and future Hall of Famer, Cal Ripken Jr.

As Junior and his younger brother Billy, who would join his brother as the Orioles' double-play combination from 1987 to 1990, recalled, their father never pushed his sons to play baseball. But it was Cal Sr.'s teachings and examples that helped make Cal Jr. a perennial All-Star and baseball's ultimate Iron Man.

In his formative years growing up in Aberdeen, Cal Jr. watched his father set life-shaping examples in dogged perseverance and toughness in finishing a job, no matter how long or painful it became.

of the varmint.

Perhaps even more impressive was the day Cal Sr. set about repairing the old snowplow he used to clean the whole neighborhood after a storm. It only took a few minutes of inspection to discern that it had a dead battery.

Gathering his sons around him, he began lecturing on the proper method to crank a balky tractor with a heavy metal rod. When this standard procedure failed, he began cranking the tractor windmill style — a dangerous method he warned his sons never to attempt.

The warning proved fateful when the metal rod flew off the snowplow and struck Cal Sr. squarely on the forehead. Blood began spurting out of the ugly wound. He covered it with an oily rag and ordered Cal Jr. to drive him home, where he quickly locked himself in the bathroom. Eventually, he emerged with several improvised butterfly bandages to stem the bleeding and a giant band-aid to keep things in place.

His sons urged him to seek proper medical attention at a nearby hospital, but showing little patience, Cal Sr.

– The Ripken Way –

THE RIPKENS: A BASEBALL FAMILY

CAL RIPKEN SR.

- FULL NAME: Calvin Edwin Ripken Sr.
- BORN: December 17, 1935
- DIED: March 25, 1999
- Cal Ripken Sr. was an Orioles coach from 1976-1986 and 1989-1992 and manager from 1987-1988.

CAL RIPKEN JR.

- FULL NAME: Calvin Edwin Ripken Jr.
- BORN: August 24, 1960
- Cal Ripken Jr. was drafted by the Orioles in the second round of the 1978 draft (48th overall selection).
- DEBUT: August 10, 1981

BILLY RIPKEN

- FULL NAME: William Oliver Ripken
- BORN: December 16, 1964
- Billy Ripken was drafted by the Orioles in the 11th round of the 1982 draft (286th overall selection).
- DEBUT: July 11, 1987
- He played seven seasons alongside Cal, 1987-1992 and 1996. Billy Ripken batted .247 with 674 hits, 121 doubles, 20 home runs and 229 RBI over his 912-game career.

demanded a ride back to the shed, where he finished the job of repairing the tractor … and proceeded to plow the whole neighborhood.

This, and other vivid instances of his father's tough resolve, was not lost on Cal Jr. At a tender age, when he would get nicked by a ground ball during a practice session at the local field, his father would bellow, "A baseball only weighs five ounces. How much can it hurt?"

It was this same tough-it-out mentality that helped keep Cal Jr. in the lineup when "The Streak" was still in its embryonic stage. In September 1983, when the Orioles were completing their drive to an American League pennant and a world championship, Cal Jr. complained to his father about a sprained left hand before a game in Minnesota. Cal Sr., then an Oriole coach, advised his son, "Put some tobacco juice on it and use your top hand when you're batting."

Father knows best. That night against the Twins, Cal Jr. collected five hits totaling 13 bases, tying an Orioles' record.

Lessons on how to play the game were ingrained at an early age when Cal Jr. would faithfully attend baseball clinics conducted by his father throughout the East Coast. On a rare occasion when Cal Sr. had an opportunity during the major league season to witness one of his son's high school games, he watched with admiration as Junior backhanded a ball deep in the hole at shortstop and threw out the hitter.

The morning after, he asked his son where he had learned to make such a difficult defensive play, and Cal Jr. calmly replied, "Remember that clinic you held last year in Rochester? That's how you instructed the infielders to make that play."

After the spring semester ended, Cal Jr. had the opportunity to participate in early workouts at Memorial Stadium, but he was only allowed to shag flies while wearing a proper uniform. "If you're out there on the field," his father said, "look like you belong."

It was difficult for Cal Jr. to blot out the distractions in 1993 when the Orioles decided his father was dispensable and his brother Billy was released before catching on with the Texas Rangers.

"I felt lost out there," he recalled in his biography, "Iron Man". "I was used to having my father and brother here for support. But the reality of the situation is that I have to do my job as a baseball player — I have to be professional."

Cal Sr. could not have said it better. The famous son put an exclamation point on his dad's "team comes first" philosophy on that September night at Camden Yards when he surpassed Lou Gehrig's record by playing in his 2,131st consecutive game.

After an emotional lap around the field to share the moment with the adoring crowd, he gathered himself for a memorable speech. At the conclusion, he said, "Whether your name is Gehrig, Ripken, DiMaggio or Robinson, or you are some youngster who picked up his bat and put on his glove, you are challenged by the game of baseball to do your very best, day in and day out, and that's all I ever tried to do."

Yes, The Ripken Way was always the right way. ☐

ALAN GOLDSTEIN IS A LONGTIME SPORTS WRITER FOR THE BALTIMORE SUN, A MEMBER OF THE MARYLAND BOXING HALL OF FAME AND A NAT FLEISCHER AWARD RECIPIENT.

CONGRATULATIONS TO A
BALTIMORE HERO.

He's one of the many reasons we're proud to be from Baltimore.

www.kbank.net

THE POWER OF K.

EQUAL OPPORTUNITY LENDER

Member FDIC

When do you know an athlete is destined for the Hall of Fame? At 6 years old? 7? 15? 20?

Little League? High School? College? Class A ball? Triple A? Impossible to know, really. What isn't, though, is a young athlete's desire, work ethic and passion to keep playing, whether he's 6 or 60.

Cal Ripken Jr.'s desire to play sports as a kid wasn't learned, it was inherited. It wasn't pushed on him, it was nurtured. With his dad, Cal Sr., working as a scout, coach and minor league manager for the Orioles, Cal spent his summers anywhere but in their Aberdeen hometown. Mom Vi Ripken would pack up the car in early June and

Cal made the varsity baseball team at Aberdeen as a freshman — as a 125-pound, 14-year-old second baseman for coach Don Morrison. Four years later, he was pitching for the Eagles in the Class A state baseball championship under coach George Connolly. Before that game the Eagles had to beat Walter's Arundel Wildcats for the District V championship. Arundel had won back-to-back state titles in 1976-77 and featured one of the area's premier pitchers in Dave Wisniewski.

"We went up to Harford County and played them," Walter said. "Cal pitched and we had a tough time with him. He had a major league slider back then and he certainly knew what he was doing."

Aberdeen won the game, 2-1. Eventually, the Eagles

THE HIGH SCHOOL YEARS

By | Keith Mills

Cal Jr., Elly, Fred and Billy would hit the road for Elmira, N.Y., Dallas/Fort Worth or Asheville, N.C., not to return until late August. The Ripkens played ball from sunup to sundown, seven days a week, 52 weeks a year.

Cal is still playing — basketball — two to three times a week at the gym in his Reisterstown home, where he may have lost a step at 46 but not in his desire and passion for a game he didn't even play in high school.

Cal was a soccer and baseball player at Aberdeen High in Harford County. He was tall and lanky, quick and powerful, smart and astute, confident and talented. He wasn't quite Roy Hobbs but Ripken was a natural, an outstanding high school athlete who everyone knew was destined for a career in Major League Baseball. He had a strong arm, quick bat, quicker hands and a makeup that oozed baseball savvy. Indeed, it wasn't long before word spread from scout to scout that Cal Sr.'s oldest boy could play.

"I remember seeing him field ground balls," said Bernie Walter, the baseball coach at Arundel High School and an associate scout to Dick Bowie, the Orioles scout who drafted and signed Cal in 1978. "He had great hands and he knew how to play. You could see that right away."

played Thomas Stone of Charles County for the state championship and Cal pitched again, though the day was not going well. He had just pitched two days earlier and trailed 3-1 in the fourth inning when heavy rains postponed the game. Three days later, the two teams played again and this time the future Oriole Iron Man was on his game, striking out 17 as the Eagles won, 7-2, to register Aberdeen's first and only baseball state championship.

A few days later Cal was drafted in the second round by the Orioles, turning down an offer from the Military Academy at West Point for soccer. Despite his passion for basketball, Cal did not play that sport at Aberdeen. Cal deferred because of his slender frame and instead played winter soccer for his father.

Ripken Sr. coached a variety of soccer teams in the Aberdeen area during the baseball offseason and it was common knowledge around Harford County that if he wasn't coaching and managing the Orioles' minor league teams, he'd be coaching soccer somewhere.

"Show me a good soccer player," Cal Sr. once said, "and I'll show you a great athlete."

Cal was not just a good soccer player, he was a great soccer player. He was a two-time captain for Terry

– The High School Years –

Colaw's Eagles, earning both All-Harford County and All-Metro honors. As a senior in the fall of 1977, he led Aberdeen into the state playoffs. Under Colaw, also the school's basketball coach, Aberdeen won the Class A soccer state championship in 1973 and was a tough, physical team in '77 when the Eagles played Andover High of Anne Arundel County in the District V Class A finals.

"Cal was very good," said Andover's Dan Krimmelbein, an assistant at that time to head coach Steve Malone, now vice president of the National Soccer Coaches Association of America. "I had seen them play earlier and their whole offense seemed to revolve around Cal. They played him up front, which I guess now you'd call a center-forward. He was so big they tried to push the ball down the sideline and cross the ball to him in the middle. He was definitely a force."

He was also a marked man that November day at Westminster High School. Billy Warren was Andover's "sweeper" that year and marked Cal all over the field. So did center halfback Alex Gerus. Andover won, 1-0, on a goal by Bobby Bates, though the Archers later lost in the state quarterfinals to Loch Raven.

"Billy was very good," Krimmelbein said. "And we were tough up the middle also and we shut them out but it was a tough, physical game."

Cal's soccer career ended in the fall of 1977. His high school baseball career ended with a state championship and a reputation as one of he best amateur players in the country. As a pitcher he struck out 100 batters in 60 innings with a 0.70 ERA at Aberdeen while leading Harford County in hitting with a .472 average with 29 RBIs.

In the summer of 1977 Cal played for the Putty Hill Optimist amateur team, a successful team coached by Marty Malloy, now baseball coach at Gilman. In August of '77, Cal led Putty Hill to a berth in the Mickey Mantle World Series in Sherman, Texas. The following June, he was on his way to Bluefield, W.Va., with fellow Baltimore prospect Tim Norris to play for the Orioles' rookie team in the Appalachian League.

Both Cal and Norris were drafted and signed by Bowie, the team's longtime area scout. Cal was the fourth player picked that year by the O's, one of four second-round selections. Robert Bryce, a third baseman from Cincinnati, was the team's No. 1 pick, followed by Larry Sheets of Staunton, Va., Edwin Hook, a pitcher from San Diego, Ripken and Cecil Whitehead, an outfielder from Valdosta State University in Georgia. Shortstop Bob Bonner, who played with Cal on the Orioles, was taken in the third round and Norris, a hard-throwing, right-handed pitcher, was selected in the fourth.

Walter was working for Bowie at that time as an associate scout and after his Wildcats played Aberdeen in the '78 state playoffs, his scouting report broke from what many scouts at that time were thinking and said to draft Cal as an infielder, not a pitcher.

"He was a very good pitcher," Walter said. "But I didn't know how much better he was going to get. He had a major league slider at that time, a good curveball and a good fastball. I just didn't know how much harder he'd throw. But as a shortstop and hitter he was excellent and I thought showed a lot more potential as an infielder.

"He would just do things at that time you didn't see a high school kid do. You could really tell he was well-schooled. I told our kids to watch him closely because he was an exceptional high school player."

Bowie, scouting director Tom Giordano and general manager Hank Peters agreed, signing Cal as a third baseman. Of course he would later move to shortstop at the suggestion of Earl Weaver, but he will forever be an Aberdeen Eagle, one of the finest high school athletes in Harford County history. □

A LONGTIME TELEVISION SPORTS REPORTER IN BALTIMORE, KEITH MILLS IS NOW A SPORTS REPORTER FOR WBAL RADIO AND A HIGH SCHOOL SPORTS COLUMNIST FOR PRESSBOX.

More than once he was compared to Jim Palmer, but it shouldn't come as a surprise why Cal Ripken Jr. preferred the infield over the mound.

As a rising star at Aberdeen High School, Ripken played every day (what else is new?), but his playing time was divided between pitching and playing the infield. For the most important games, the ones that attracted the scouts, he invariably could be found on the mound, which helps explain why his baseball grades were about curveballs and control rather than hitting and fielding.

Many years ago, while discussing the decision that was made about the direction of his career, Ripken routinely

more than a rangy right-hander with a smooth delivery. "I think he will hit and can play in the big leagues — and I'm not convinced he can't play shortstop," Bowie said two months before Ripken began his senior season in high school.

It was Bowie's diligence, perhaps more than anything, that fueled Ripken's path to the big leagues. Bowie may have been the only scout who filed reports on games when Cal Jr. wasn't pitching, checking out Ripken's range and arm strength while also getting more looks at him as a hitter.

Joe Branzell, who ran a strong amateur program in Washington, D.C. and scouted the mid-Atlantic area for the Senators and Rangers, and Joe Consoli, longtime

THE BEST PITCHER YOU NEVER SAW

By Jim Henneman

explained his affinity for pitching. Simply put, he liked the idea of being in the middle of the action, and on any given day the mound was the place to be.

"When you're pitching, you're in control of the game on every pitch," Ripken said. "It's the best place to be — but you can only be there once every four or five days. As a kid I was a catcher, because 'Pops' (Cal Sr.) was a catcher and you always want to be like your dad — plus, that seemed like the second-best place to be. But I stopped catching early, probably because the equipment was too big, and after that, shortstop seemed like the third-best place to be."

As it turned out, there were probably only two people who believed, at least initially, that Ripken had the tools to play in the middle of the infield — and you would be hard-pressed to determine which had the greater influence on his career.

The first was Dick Bowie, the Orioles' scout who saw

scout for the Pirates, shared almost identical scouting reports (including occasional "Ripkin" misspellings) with this writer more than 15 years ago — on Ripken's 10th anniversary in the big leagues.

Both scouts projected Ripken to top out with an average fastball, possibly above-average changeup and control and both gave him high marks on the intangibles. "Built like and has Jim Palmer actions," Branzell said. He also noted that Ripken "swings bat pretty good."

Consoli called Ripken a "fine-looking, long-armed, big-boned, physical specimen" who had "sneaky stuff" and was an "outstanding competitor." Both scouts noted Ripken's youth (he was 17), relative inexperience and his background as the son of a major league coach, Cal Sr. Branzell listed Ripken's potential bonus value at $20,000, while Consoli had him pegged in the $8,000 range.

"Looking back now, you realize he pitched every big

– The Best Pitcher You Never Saw –

game," Branzell recalled years later. "I never saw him play the infield. The fact that he was playing shortstop when he wasn't pitching probably took something away from his arm at both positions. That's something that might not have been taken into consideration at the time. He only threw about average for me, but you had to think he'd get faster — and you had to be crazy not to like his makeup.

"I don't turn in a report unless I think a kid is a prospect, and I'm conservative," Branzell said. "I put down $20,000 and that was good money in those days, so I must've liked him. I definitely think the Orioles had an advantage. They weren't going to take the chance of missing out on the son of Cal Sr."

It wasn't hard for young Ripken to figure out what the scouts were thinking. "At first (early in his high school career) there would be two or four scouts at a game, then it got to be six, eight or 10, and at the end there were a lot of them," Ripken recalled years after becoming established in the big leagues. "They always seemed to make sure to come around when I pitched, and a lot of times they wanted to see me throw on the side — but nobody came around and wanted to see me take ground balls or hit in batting practice.

"It got to the point where I was sure I was going to be drafted, but I wasn't sure I would be drafted the way I wanted to be. It kind of scared me, disappointed me in a way, but it was out of my control."

But not necessarily out of the control of Cal Sr. During Cal Jr.'s senior year in high school, the two Ripkens mapped a simple plan about his immediate future. "When the colleges started coming around, Dad and I talked mostly about whether I was going to pursue a career in baseball. If I had the ability (which would probably be reflected by his position in the draft), the feeling was to get on with it and if it didn't work out, start over again in college. I agreed with that … I was prepared to play."

As for what position Cal Jr. would play, that would be up to others, but Cal Sr. later revealed his son actually held the trump card. "I didn't talk to any scouts before the draft," Cal Sr. said immediately after the Orioles took his son on the second round in 1978. "When Tom Giordano (then the Orioles' scouting director) asked, 'What do you want to do?' I told him it wasn't what I wanted to do, it was what Cal Jr. wanted to do — and he wanted to play every day."

Little did anyone know at the time that "every day" would translate into 2,632 straight games.

Even though every other team surveyed (and there were many) had Cal Jr. ranked as a second- or third-round pick — as a pitcher — Cal Sr. indicated that wouldn't have happened without a full trial as a position player. "Had another team drafted him, that (a full trial as a position player) would have been a stipulation before he signed," Cal Sr. said at the time. "Our thinking was that if something happened, he could always go back to pitching when he was 20 or 21 years old. But if he started out pitching and didn't hit or field for three or four years, it would be difficult to go back to playing every day."

Fortunately for everyone concerned, push never came to shove when it came time for a decision. Bowie had the advantage of taking Cal Jr. to Memorial Stadium for a private workout.

"I don't remember how long it was before the draft, but Cal had about a week to 10 days to rest (his arm) after his season ended," said Jim Gilbert, a part-time scout at the time who took over the territory after Bowie's death three years later. "We had seen enough of him as a pitcher and Dick liked his bat and wanted to see his arm from shortstop when it was fully rested.

"Clyde Kluttz (then director of player development)

– The Best Pitcher You Never Saw –

told Dick, 'When you get finished, come back to the office and tell me whether he's going to be a position player or a pitcher.' Dick, his son Randy, (associate scouts) Paul McNeil and Bill Timberlake and myself were the only ones there."

Bowie saw enough in the workout to confirm his original judgment. He told Kluttz he felt Cal Jr. should be drafted as an infielder. The rest is history.

Once Ripken got to the big leagues it was manager Earl Weaver, in his constant search for power in the lineup, who became convinced Ripken could play shortstop, though possibly at some personal expense. Noting that Robin Yount, who hadn't yet made his transition to center field, and Alan Trammell were still in their primes, Weaver made one of the worst observations of his career. "I probably ruined the kid's chances of ever making an All-Star team," he said.

It didn't quite work out that way, and in retrospect the move proved to be a defining moment for two Hall of Famers, even though it was met at first with more than a little skepticism.

Weaver left himself open to criticism because the Orioles had traded Doug DeCinces to create a spot at third base and there was considerable speculation that the youngster didn't have the range for the position. Weaver allayed those fears with a single piece of advice to the rookie which became the foundation for the defensive excellence Ripken would develop.

"He told me, 'Make sure you catch the ball and throw it straight — the worst that can happen is there will be a man on first,' and I never forgot that," Ripken later said about the transition.

But what about what might have been? Suppose Bowie (who, by the way, did consider Ripken a pitching prospect) had been wrong about him being a position player — and the others had been right?

Ripken doesn't know. "Most players in the big leagues pitched somewhere along the line, and they all think they could do it," he said. "I would like to think I would have been successful, but that's something we'll never know."

Neither will anyone else, but the guy he was once compared to had an idea when the subject was first broached to him. "Can I visualize what he'd be like as a pitcher?" Palmer asked in response to a query. "Yeah, I can ... he'd be throwing four or five different pitches for strikes, he'd probably sidearm hitters, and you know he'd be a great fielder."

Former manager Johnny Oates may have made the most astute observation. "I know this — he's got the best screwball on the team right now. He'll throw it on the sideline while warming up and the bottom drops out," Oates said during the first year of his run as Orioles' manager.

"I wonder though, if he'd know as much about the game as he does now if he was a pitcher," Oates said. "There is just so much more to cope with (as a shortstop)."

Which, undoubtedly, is why Ripken preferred the position, "the third-best place to be," and left others to wonder if he might not have been the best pitcher the Orioles never saw. ☐

JIM HENNEMAN IS A VETERAN WRITER WHO HAS SERVED AS PRESIDENT OF THE BASEBALL WRITERS' ASSOCIATION OF AMERICA.

TOP 48 PICKS IN THE 1978 DRAFT

#	Player	#	Player	#	Player	#	Player
1	Bob Horner (1978-88))	11	Rod Boxberger	21	Gerry Aubin	35	Edwin Hook
2	Lloyd Moseby (1980-1991)	12	Kirk Gibson (1979-1995)	22	Robert Boyce	36	Chris Bando (1981-1989)
3	Hubie Brooks (1980-1994)	13	Bill Hayes (1980-1981)	23	Rip Rollins	37	Danny Heep (1979-1991)
4	Mike Morgan (1978-2002)	14	Tom Brunansky (1981-1994)	24	Matt Winters (1989-1989)	38	Craig Johnson
5	Andy Hawkins (1982 -1991)	15	Bob Hicks	25	Buddy Biancalana (1982-1987)	39	Mel Hall (1981-1996)
6	Tito Nanni	16	Lenny Faedo (1980-1984)	26	Brian Ryder	40	Doug Gwosdz (1981-1984)
7	Bob Cummings	17	Nick Esasky (1983-1990)	27	Matt Sinatro (1981-1992)	41	David Kable
8	Nick Hernandez	18	Rex Hudler (1984-1998)	28	Tim Thompson	42	Mike Riley
9	Glenn Franklin	19	Brad Garnett	29	Larry Sheets (1984-1993)	43	Dave Van Gorder
10	Phil Lansford	20	Tim Conroy (1978-1987)	30	Keith Atherton (1983-1989)	44	Buck Belue
				31	David White	45	Brad Palmer
				32	Dave Valle (1984-1996)	46	Amos Lewis
				33	Steve Raine	47	Clay Smith
				34	Rich Naumann	48	Cal Ripken (1981-2001)

(YEARS IN MAJORS)

FROM ABERDEEN TO COOPERSTOWN

By | Jim Henneman

As the Baltimore Oriole might fly, the shortest distance between Aberdeen, Md., and Cooperstown, N.Y., is 284.82 miles, but anybody making the drive is more likely to travel 319.84 miles to get there almost two hours faster.

Even MapQuest knows there are no short cuts to the home of baseball's Hall of Fame.

And nobody understands that better than Cal Ripken Jr., Aberdeen's favorite son and a 2007 inductee into what has been called the most elite fraternity in sports. The path that Ripken followed required most of a lifetime and a dedication to a game that was as much an avocation as it was the family profession.

What made this journey so unique was the fact that virtually every step of the way, on every rung of the minor league ladder, he was escorted by a mentor who was the most influential person in his career. Cal Ripken Jr., like his sister and two brothers, literally grew up in the minor leagues, where Cal Ripken Sr. raised a family that would eventually include a Hall of Famer.

"Senior," as he was affectionately known by thousands

"YOU CAN'T REALLY MAKE IT TO THE BIG LEAGUES UNLESS YOU HAVE TALENT, BUT COUPLED WITH THAT IS YOUR WORK AND YOUR DESIRE."

– Cal Ripken Jr. –

of players who came through the Orioles' system, was the ultimate organization man. He was the first player ever signed by scout Walter Youse, hired on because the team needed a catcher at what was then the Class C level, somebody who knew the game and could handle a young pitching staff.

His playing career was destined to be sporadic, but from Day One Senior was tabbed as coach/manager/teacher material. In a touch of irony, his best season as a player was also his last — 1960, the year Cal Jr. was born. He hit .281, with nine home runs and 74 runs batted in for Class B Fox Cities, and years later Earl Weaver, his manager at the time, would recall: "Rip was having an MVP year, but his numbers fell off after Vi went back home to have the baby."

Weaver would reap the benefits 22 years later, as he was closing the first stage of his career as Orioles' manager, and Cal Ripken Jr. was making his mark as the American League's Rookie of the Year.

The year after his namesake was born, Cal Sr. began a 14-year minor league managing career at Leesburg, Fla., meaning Cal Jr. was still in a crib when his exposure to minor league baseball began.

– From Aberdeen To Cooperstown –

The tour would include stops in Appleton, Wis. (Fox Cities) in 1962; Aberdeen, S.D., 1963-64; Tri-Cities, 1965; Miami, Fla., 1967; Elmira, N.Y., 1968; Rochester, N.Y., 1969-70; Dallas, Texas, 1971; and Asheville, N.C., 1972-74.

It was during the last of the three summers in Asheville, his dad's final minor league season, that young Cal first crossed paths with Eddie Murray, who would not only be a future teammate, but a playing mentor who preceded him on the journey to Cooperstown.

By then a fast-developing and quick-learning 14-year-old, Cal Jr. began nourishing some illusions of the future. Along the way he had been a constant tag-a-long whenever his dad gave a clinic, and eventually he grew into a uniform and participated in on-field activities on a regular basis.

For the youngster, it was like taking graduate courses in advance while having the advantage of a personal tutor available on call. By the time Cal Sr. moved into a scouting position in 1975, a year before re-joining Weaver as a coach for the Orioles, young Cal had developed enough to give indications that there was indeed a prime prospect in the making.

Away from his personal and parental on-field tutelage for the first time, Ripken blossomed into a double prospect — as a pitcher and a position player — and ultimately became a second-round draft choice of the Orioles in June of 1978, two months before his 18th birthday. At this stage, after an interval of four years, Cal Sr. took part in the decision-making process, on two fronts.

The first resulted in the decision, if he was deemed good enough to be a high-round selection in the amateur draft, to put college on hold and proceed immediately with a baseball career. The second was whether he should pitch or play the infield — and it was Senior's strong belief that playing every day should be the first preference (and how prophetic was that?), figuring it would present the easiest way to switch down the road if necessary. As it turned out, that proved to be a moot point as the Orioles, based on the recommendation of scout Dick Bowie, are believed to be the only team that ranked him higher as a position player.

Reflecting on that exciting time of his life, after signing his first professional contract (which called for a bonus of $20,000 plus incentive clauses for advancement above Class A that totaled $7,500), Ripken revealed that his goals were not unlike many others. "I had the same dreams that everybody [who played] did," he said. "It was just the next step of the dream.

"The funny part was, when Dad managed in the minor

– From Aberdeen To Cooperstown –

leagues, my goal was to be a minor-league player. I mean, even though I knew the big leagues, I still thought being a minor-league player was the best job that you could get… you got paid to play… some people cared about you. It was small-time for some, but to me it seemed pretty cool."

What Ripken quickly realized, of course, was that he had already lived part of the dream, blazing the minor league trail with his dad/mentor, and now the dream shifted into overdrive. Ask him what he expected at that point and the dedication, the passion, the desire for excellence come through, complete with an all too simple explanation that sounds like it could have been written by the U.S. Army.

"The goal is to be all that you can be," he said. "You have to fulfill your potential. You can't really make it to the big leagues unless you have talent, but coupled with that is your work and your desire. The hard part is you don't know how good you can be, because there are different levels — quite honestly there are probably six, seven or eight levels between your high school days and your big league days — and they get harder with each one. I just wanted to be the best that I could be."

As his career developed, it turned out that the best Ripken could be was to be one of only eight men in history to record 3,000 hits and 400 home runs; to start 17 straight All-Star games; to be the only player to win Rookie of the Year and Most Valuable Player awards in back-to-back years; to set records by making only three errors in an entire season, with a .996 fielding percentage; and to play 95 consecutive games (431 chances) without an error.

And then, of course, there was something about a streak of 2,632 straight games played.

He will forever be linked to that streak, but in reality his dedication to, knowledge of and ability to absorb the nuances of the game were Ripken's true trademarks. His idol growing up, quite naturally, was Brooks Robinson, the Hall of Fame third baseman, and the guy who taught him the most about playing shortstop was Mark Belanger. Eventually, he would make his own mark at both positions.

"Growing up, Brooksie was a teacher by example," he said. "You could learn a lot just watching him, and nobody handled himself better — I still haven't found a person who said anything bad about Brooksie.

"Mark was a teacher by words and example," said Ripken,

CAL RIPKEN JR. CAREER AWARDS

1982: AL Rookie of the Year

1983: AL MVP

1991: AL MVP

1992: Lou Gehrig Memorial Award

1992: Roberto Clemente Award

CAL RIPKEN FINISHED IN THE TOP 10 IN BATTING AVERAGE THREE TIMES DURING HIS CAREER:

1983: Ranked fifth in the AL with .318 average

1984: Ranked ninth in the AL with .304 average

1991: Ranked sixth in the AL with .323 average

GOLD GLOVES:

1991 (AL-SS)   1992 (AL-SS)

SILVER SLUGGERS:

1983-AL-SS	1984-AL-SS	1985-AL-SS
1986-AL-SS	1989-AL-SS	1991-AL-SS
1993-AL-SS	1994-AL-SS	

* The Silver Slugger Awards are given each year to the best offensive player at each position in each league.

ALL-STAR:

1991 All-Star Game MVP   1991 Home Run Derby Champion

2001 All-Star Game MVP

* Cal Ripken Jr. is the only AL player to have won the All-Star Game MVP Award twice. Three NL players have done so – Willie Mays (1963 and 1968), Steve Garvey (1974 and 1976) and Gary Carter (1981 and 1984).
* Ripken also participated in the Home Run Derby at the 1985 and 1992 All-Star Games.

who benefited from many hands-on sessions while still in high school and Cal Sr. was an Orioles' coach. "Belanger was a great teacher … I don't know if people understand that. He was technical in his angles and in his understanding of the position. I don't know too many people who understood shortstop the way he did. I was the recipient of that knowledge because he took an interest in me, and I was able to be around him. At 14, he was telling me things about going into the hole, and backhanding off of your throwing leg, or taking an angle to the ball.

"I couldn't understand it, because I didn't have the wealth of experience, but I listened to the words and as I played the game, there were times when I understood what he was talking about. When I first came up (in 1981, and not playing a lot) he was still there... I sat with him a lot and he would point out things that other short-stops were doing. I specifically remember him pointing out Alan Trammell (whom Ripken has often said he patterned himself after) and telling me to watch him."

Though they gave decidedly different appearances, the reed-thin Belanger and the more robust Ripken actually had very similar styles. Belanger was quicker, Ripken more powerfully built, but both had soft hands, graceful strides and fluid motions that more often than not made plays look routine.

Citing the presence of Trammell and Robin Yount at the position, Weaver made one of the poorest observations of his career during Ripken's rookie year in 1982. "With those two guys (Trammell and Yount) around,

> ℞
>
> "PRACTICE DOESN'T MAKE PERFECT ... PERFECT PRACTICE MAKES PERFECT."
>
> – Cal Ripken Sr. –

the kid may never get to play in an All-Star game," Weaver said. It didn't quite work out that way — due at least in part because Ripken was a good student.

Nothing makes a teacher look better than a good pupil. And there is hardly a better learning experience than on-the-job training, which is what Ripken was getting throughout that trek through the minor leagues. His father/mentor was a guy who lived by a motto that insisted "practice doesn't make perfect... perfect practice makes perfect."

Somehow you get the idea that if Senior had been a cabinet maker, the kid would have been making exquisite furniture. And, like the trip from Aberdeen to Cooperstown, there would be no short cuts. □

JIM HENNEMAN IS A VETERAN WRITER WHO HAS SERVED AS PRESIDENT OF THE BASEBALL WRITERS' ASSOCIATION OF AMERICA.

CAL RIPKEN CAREER STATISTICS

Regular Season

Year	G	AB	R	H	2B	3B	HR	RBI	BB	SO	SB	OBP	SLG	AVG
1981	23	39	1	5	0	0	0	0	1	8	0	.150	.128	.128
1982	160	598	90	158	32	5	28	93	46	95	3	.317	.475	.264
1983	162	663	121	211	47	2	27	102	58	97	0	.371	.517	.318
1984	162	641	103	195	37	7	27	86	71	89	2	.374	.510	.304
1985	161	642	116	181	32	5	26	110	67	68	2	.347	.469	.282
1986	162	627	98	177	35	1	25	81	70	60	4	.355	.461	.282
1987	162	624	97	157	28	3	27	98	81	77	3	.333	.436	.252
1988	161	575	87	152	25	1	23	81	102	69	2	.372	.431	.264
1989	162	646	80	166	30	0	21	93	57	72	3	.317	.401	.257
1990	161	600	78	150	28	4	21	84	82	66	3	.341	.415	.250
1991	162	650	99	210	46	5	34	114	53	46	6	.374	.566	.323
1992	162	637	73	160	29	1	14	72	64	50	4	.323	.366	.251
1993	162	641	87	165	26	3	24	90	65	58	1	.329	.420	.257
1994	112	444	71	140	19	3	13	75	32	41	1	.364	.459	.315
1995	144	550	71	144	33	2	17	88	52	59	0	.324	.422	.262
1996	163	640	94	178	40	1	26	102	59	78	1	.341	.466	.278
1997	162	615	79	166	30	0	17	84	56	73	1	.331	.402	.270
1998	161	601	65	163	27	1	14	61	51	68	0	.331	.389	.271
1999	86	332	51	113	27	0	18	57	13	31	0	.368	.584	.340
2000	83	309	43	79	16	0	15	56	23	37	0	.310	.453	.256
2001	128	477	43	114	16	0	14	68	26	63	0	.276	.361	.239
Totals:	3,001	11,551	1,647	3,184	603	44	431	1,695	1,129	1,305	36	.340	.447	.276

Postseason

Year	Round	Opp.	W/L	G	AB	R	H	2B	3B	HR	RBI	BB	SO	SB	OBP	SLG	AVG
1983	ALCS	CHW	W	4	15	5	6	2	0	0	1	2	3	0	.500	.533	.400
1983	WS	PHI	W	5	18	2	3	0	0	0	1	3	4	0	.286	.167	.167
1996	ALDS	CLE	W	4	18	2	8	3	0	0	2	0	3	0	.474	.611	.444
1996	ALCS	NYY	L	5	20	1	5	1	0	0	0	1	4	0	.286	.300	.250
1997	ALDS	SEA	W	4	16	1	7	2	0	0	1	2	2	0	.500	.562	.438
1997	ALCS	CLE	L	6	23	3	8	2	0	1	3	4	6	0	.444	.565	.348
Totals:				28	110	14	37	10	0	1	8	12	22	0	.411	.455	.336

NO CUSTOMER COMEBACKS.
NOW THAT'S A VICTORY.

Bendix is putting an end to customer comebacks. Low dust. Virtually no noise.

Just a full line of products thoroughly tested to perform across all vehicle types.

Want high-quality parts that meet all of your needs? Grab the blue box.

A **Honeywell** car care product.   www.bendixbrakes.com
©2006 Honeywell International Inc.

Bendix® True blue.
by Honeywell

Bendix congratulates Cal Ripken, our hometown hero!

AAP Auto Parts
410-643-6400

Action Automotive
410-866-5900

Annapolis Auto Parts
410-268-6615

Autocraft
410-877-7990

County Auto Parts
410-252-0820

Mainline Auto Parts
410-367-5000

North Point Auto Supply
410-284-0800

Nor-Lin Auto Parts
410-789-6220

Westway Auto Parts
410-788-5533

KEEPING CAL IN THE GAME

By | Mike Lurie

As Cal Ripken circled Oriole Park on Sept. 6, 1995, celebrating with fans after his 2,131st straight game became official, longtime club trainer Richie Bancells took in the scene with unique perspective.

Bancells' first day in pro baseball was the same as Ripken's. They experienced their inaugural opening day together in 1978, as members of the Orioles' Appalachian Rookie League affiliate in Bluefield, W.Va. Therefore, few people — besides Cal Sr. and Bill Ripken — could say they had known Cal Jr. in a baseball setting this long.

"The night of 2,131 was kind of a blur," Bancells said. "But the thing that made me most proud of him and proud of our friendship, was when he circled the stadium that night — it showed the kind of person he is.

"I remember thinking back to how our first day in pro ball coincided and how, since Bluefield back in 1978, nothing about him had changed. He never changed in terms of how he felt about people and treated people."

As Ripken came up through the Orioles' system, he quickly displayed a thorough attention to detail on training matters.

"One of the things that was unique about him, and it went back to Triple-A, is that he was one of the first ballplayers I had [worked with] who had a keen interest in his body and how it functioned," Bancells said. "He'd want to know, 'What makes this work?' and 'What makes that work?'

"He was constantly asking me questions about the body and how something would work for him. You would think most

"ONE THING THAT MADE ME PROUD WAS HOW MUCH HE TRUSTED ME."

– Richie Bancells –

athletes, since their body is their investment, would have a bigger interest in these issues. But not all of them do."

No one knows that better than Tim Bishop, who joined the Orioles in 1993 as strength and conditioning coach. That was the year of the infamous Sunday brawl with the Seattle Mariners, a Camden Yards melee from which Ripken emerged with a badly injured knee. It was one of the few threats to the streak that Ripken experienced.

"Obviously, that was the most publicized issue. But what sticks out to me is all the other little things that added up," said Bishop, who left the organization late in the 2006 season to establish his own personal training company. "What the reporters didn't see was him on a training table when he was sick, or the black-and-blue marks all over his body just from the toll the game takes on you.

"But when it was time for BP (batting practice), he was just ready to go."

Bishop considers Ripken something of an innovator in terms of baseball conditioning.

"One of the things we started doing was some interval sprinting on the treadmill. When he started getting toward the end of his career, that was a way of just keeping his legs under him," Bishop said. "Cal was always ahead of his time. Now, every organization, I would guess, does interval training when its players run on the treadmill or outside. [Interval training helps athletes do] well in explosive power sports, I think that is why Cal played basketball in the offseason.

"There were many, many nights after a long day and a long night game, and after he signed autographs, that Cal and I

– Keeping Cal In The Game –

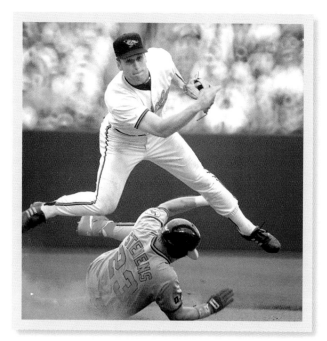

would go out on the field after a game. It could be after midnight and he would do some of those sprints on the field."

Both Bishop and Bancells can attest to early-morning visits at Ripken's home in the offseason, be it for conditioning purposes or to work through the serious back problems Ripken experienced late in his career. They encountered a man who conveyed a strong appreciation for his family, a fervent interest in what would best advance his training goals, and a real sense of trust in the two men who helped keep him in peak condition.

"One thing that made me proud was how much he trusted me," Bancells said. "If I said to him, 'Cal, go stand on your head in the corner of the locker room for 20 minutes, it'll make your knee better,' he would have looked at me funny, but he would have done it." □

A LONGTIME SPORTS WRITER FOR NEWSPAPERS AND THE WEB, MIKE LURIE IS CURRENTLY A SPORTS REPORTER ON WYPR RADIO AND WORKS IN INSTITUTIONAL ADVANCEMENT AT UMBC.

CONSECUTIVE GAMES PLAYED

NAME	GAMES	FIRST GAME	LAST GAME	TEAM
Cal Ripken Jr.	2,632	May 30, 1982	September 19, 1998	Orioles
Sachio Kinugasa	2,215	October 19, 1970	October 22, 1987	Hiroshima Carp (Japan)
Lou Gehrig	2,130	June 1, 1925	April 30, 1939	Yankees
Everett Scott	1,307	June 20, 1916	May 5, 1925	Red Sox, Yankees
Steve Garvey	1,207	September 3, 1975	July 29, 1983	Dodgers, Padres
Billy Williams	1,117	September 22, 1963	September 2, 1970	Cubs
Joe Sewell	1,103	September 13, 1922	April 30, 1930	Indians
Miguel Tejada	1,080	June 2, 2000	Active	Athletics, Orioles
Stan Musial	895	April 15, 1952	August 23, 1957	Cardinals
Eddie Yost	829	April 30, 1949	May 11, 1955	Senators
Gus Suhr	822	September 11, 1931	June 4, 1937	Pirates
Nellie Fox	798	August 8, 1955	September 3, 1960	White Sox
Pete Rose	745	September 2, 1978	August 23, 1983	Reds, Phillies
Dale Murphy	740	September 26, 1981	July 8, 1986	Braves
Richie Ashburn	730	June 7, 1950	April 13, 1955	Phillies
Ernie Banks	717	August 28, 1956	June 22, 1961	Cubs
Mark Teixeira	436	May 21, 2004	Active	Rangers
Ichiro Suzuki	391	July 11, 2004	Active	Mariners
Carlos Lee	325	September 23, 2004	Active	White Sox, Brewers, Rangers
Bobby Abreu	311	September 29, 2004	Active	Phillies, Yankees

⊢ * AS LISTED ON BASEBALL-ALMANAC.COM ⊣

On the night of Sept. 20, 1998, Orioles manager Ray Miller did what baseball managers do before every major league game — he made out his lineup. And he did it the same way that Earl Weaver, Joe Altobelli, Cal Ripken Sr., Frank Robinson, Johnny Oates, Phil Regan and Davey Johnson did it before him.

He wrote in Cal Ripken Jr.'s name in the lineup.

Sometimes, though, when a player gets to the ballpark and there is a problem — an injury, any host of issues — the manager has to make a change in his lineup. No big deal. But when Cal Ripken walks into your office shortly before game time and says he would just as soon sit this one out, it is more than a big deal. It is history. Then again, any move a manager made involving Ripken was like a

end it, it's up to you.' He said, 'Yes, and there's no sense talking about it. I just think now is the time for a number of reasons.'"

So Miller approached rookie Ryan Minor in the dugout and said, "Get your glove, you're playing third base."

Minor looked stunned and answered, "Does he know?" Miller laughed and said, "Yeah, he knows."

And so did the sports world when Minor took third base in place of Ripken. It was front-page news.

- - - - - - - - - -

It wasn't front-page news when Weaver first put Ripken in a game as a pinch-runner for Ken Singleton on Aug. 10, 1981, shortly after being called up from Triple-A Rochester after the players' strike was settled. Still, it was news because Ripken was already a heralded

MANAGING AN ICON

By | Thom Loverro

seismic event, and while he was in many ways a manager's dream — an intelligent, talented player who wanted to play every day — managing him created a unique pressure, particularly as The Streak grew.

Miller was the first Oriole manager in 16 years to put a team out on the field without Ripken. Starting on May 29, 1982, Ripken played in every single Orioles game, most of them at shortstop. On Sept. 20, 1998, Ripken's streak ended with an astounding 2,632 consecutive games played — having passed the legendary Iron Horse, Lou Gehrig, and his seemingly unbreakable record of 2,130 straight games three years earlier.

"There was really no prelude to him sitting down," Miller said. "I had written his name in the lineup and was sitting in my office going over the opposing pitchers and the hitting matchups, and he walked in no more than five to 10 minutes before the umpires were going to come out for the game and said, 'Me and the wife sat down last night and decided today's the day.' I said, 'Are you sure?' He said, 'Yes.'

"I said, 'Cal, it's an unbelievable thing. You're going to

high school baseball star from Aberdeen who grew up in the Oriole family — his father, Cal Sr., managed in the organization's minor league system for 15 years and had been a coach on Weaver's staff since 1976.

When he began putting Ripken in the lineup on a regular basis in May 1982, first at third base and then later at shortstop, Weaver had no idea that he would become part of something so remarkable and historic. After all, he was just putting a 22-year-old kid in the lineup every day, and there was nothing particularly unusual about that. By the time Weaver retired the first time after the 1982 season, Ripken had only played in 117 straight games.

Weaver's successor, Joe Altobelli, was probably the first manager who had to deal with the uniqueness of Ripken's determination to play every day, and Altobelli said he came close to breaking the streak within The Streak — Ripken's consecutive-inning streak — several times.

"It was the last two innings of a game at home, and we were losing big one night," Altobelli said. "I said to him, 'Why don't you sit these last two?' And he said, 'I'm okay, Joe. I can do these last two sitting on my head.' So I didn't

– Managing An Icon –

take him out. It happened once more, and he said again, 'No, I'll play.'

"So one day I called him in my office and said, 'What is it, why do you want to play the whole game?'" Altobelli said.

"His answer was a good one. He said when he first came up, he had to sit on the bench, back in 1981, and he said, 'I promised myself while I was sitting on that bench that if I ever got in the lineup, I would never beg out.' That was good enough for me. It was exactly what you want your players to say, and he held to it, no doubt about it."

Both streaks — consecutive innings and games — would continue through the rest of Altobelli's tenure and when Weaver came back during the 1985 season and retired again after 1986. Ironically, it would be Ripken's father, Cal Sr., who broke his son's consecutive-inning streak record — 8,243 innings, spanning 904 games. His father, then managing the Orioles, took Ripken out of the lineup in the bottom of the eighth inning on Sept. 14, 1987, sending out Ron Washington to replace him defensively, in an 18-3 beating by the Blue Jays.

By the time Frank Robinson took over as Orioles'

manager in 1988, the questions had begun about Ripken's streak — whether or not it was best for him or the club to be playing every day. Robinson said there was no doubt in his mind that his team had the best chance to win, game after game, with Ripken in the lineup, even if he was slumping.

"I could write his name down when I got to the ballpark and know he was going to go out and play," Robinson said. "He may not have been hitting, but I knew he was going to play outstanding defense and do some things on the field to help you try to win a ball game. I wished I had nine guys like that. That was the way I approached it."

When the late Johnny Oates took over in 1991, Ripken was at 1,411 consecutive games, second only to Gehrig but still a long way from the record. Oates, a backup catcher most of his playing career who knew the Ripken family well, was not about to be the manager to sit Cal.

Neither was Oates' successor in 1995, Phil Regan, whose stature as manager was certainly dwarfed by his losing record, along with the fact that he was the manager during historic 1995 when Ripken, on Sept. 6 at Camden Yards, would break Gehrig's record. Regan was a bit player that year, and owner Peter Angelos fired the manager

– Managing An Icon –

after the team posted a 71-73 record that season.

Angelos hired former Orioles second baseman Davey Johnson, one of the game's most successful managers who had led the New York Mets to the 1986 World Series championship. Johnson was the first manager to publicly butt heads with Ripken and try to change the perceived culture that the team revolved around Ripken and The Streak. In 1996, Johnson took on the task of moving Ripken from shortstop, where he had played since 1982, to third base, facing the issue that Ripken had lost too much range to stay at shortstop.

"It was a very difficult thing," Johnson said. "You had a situation where you have a first-ballot Hall of Fame guy, arguably the best shortstop in the history of the game, and it's not something you want to mess with. We had Manny Alexander, who had some physical tools as a young shortstop, and you try to get all your players in the game to see what they can do. That is part of using all 25 of them. You can't just put him in there one day, because Cal is going to play every day. I wanted to get him in the lineup and add some speed, which we didn't have."

Johnson first caused a furor by taking Ripken out of a game against the New York Yankees in the ninth inning and putting in Alexander as a pinch runner. Alexander responded by getting picked off first base. Then Johnson, answering questions from reporters, acknowledged that he was thinking about moving Ripken to third base and giving Alexander playing time at shortstop. He did so, playing Alexander for six games in July — he batted just .118. The experiment ended for the remainder of the 1996 season, as Johnson moved Ripken back to shortstop. But the Orioles, this time with Ripken's blessing, signed shortstop Mike Bordick in the offseason and Ripken moved to third base for good in 1997.

Johnson said his move to bump Ripken to third base was psychological as much as it was strategic. "I think it sent a message to the rest of the club that there is nothing sacred about anybody's position on the field, and if I could do something to make us better, I was going to consider it," he said.

Johnson also wanted to put a stop to everything going through Cal. "He didn't need that burden; to solve everyone else's problems," Johnson said. "I think it cleared the air, and let them know if they had a beef, they needed to come to me to talk about it. I think by being candid ... you have to have 25 guys contribute, and one guy shouldn't have

CAL RIPKEN JR.'S MANAGERS

DURING CAL'S STREAK

1982:	Earl Weaver, 94-68	1989:	Frank Robinson, 87-75
1983:	Joe Altobelli, 98-64	1990:	Frank Robinson, 76-85
1984:	Joe Altobelli, 85-77	1991:	Frank Robinson, 13-24
1985:	Joe Altobelli, 29-26		Johnny Oates, 54-71
	Cal Ripken, Sr., 1-0		(O's record in 1991: 67-95)
	Earl Weaver, 53-52	1992:	Johnny Oates, 89-73
	(O's record in 1985: 83-78)	1993:	Johnny Oates, 85-77
1986:	Earl Weaver, 73-89	1994:	Johnny Oates, 63-49
1987:	Cal Ripken, Sr., 67-95	1995:	Phil Regan, 71-73
1988:	Cal Ripken, Sr., 0-6	1996:	Davey Johnson, 88-74
	Frank Robinson, 54-101	1997:	Davey Johnson, 98-64
	(O's record in 1988: 54-107)	1998:	Ray Miller, 79-83

DURING CAL'S CAREER

1981:	Earl Weaver, 59-46	2000:	Mike Hargrove, 74-88
1999:	Ray Miller, 78-84	2001:	Mike Hargrove, 63-98

to carry the failure or success of the ball club. I certainly didn't want that with Cal. He was too great a player."

Ultimately, it was Ripken himself who made the decision to sit down when he went to Miller. He had been struggling with back problems since 1997 and in the end Ripken proved to be human. His last manager, Mike Hargrove, who took over the club in 2000, was faced not with managing The Streak, but managing the exit of Cal Ripken, who retired at the end of the 2001 season.

"The most difficult thing was dealing with his health and when to play him," Hargrove said. "I left it up to him and told him to let me know when he could play and couldn't play. In fact, the last two months of the season, he and I mapped out the remaining games of when he would play and wouldn't play, and we stayed pretty close to that. But there were times when his back was bothering him and he would sit out."

Even when he had planned to sit out, Ripken was still prepared to play.

"He was always very prepared and was all about winning," Hargrove said. "You have to respect that." ☐

THOM LOVERRO IS A COLUMNIST FOR THE WASHINGTON TIMES AND HAS PUBLISHED SEVERAL BOOKS, INCLUDING "HOME OF THE GAME: THE STORY OF CAMDEN YARDS".

At the end of the 1996 baseball season the Orioles front office made the decision that Cal Ripken Jr. had played his last year as an everyday shortstop.

The consecutive-game streak would still be intact, but Ripken would go through a position switch from shortstop to third base. The transition would be anything but easy — for Ripken, for the team, for the man who was going to take his place at shortstop.

Enter Mike Bordick.

Bordick had played his first seven seasons in the big leagues with the Oakland Athletics, while establishing himself as one of the game's better defensive shortstops.

"We had a young shortstop named Manny Alexander and he had no chance to play unless he played short. There was no other position where you could get him in the lineup. If Cal could play third — and we really didn't have a third baseman — I could work Alexander into the lineup. I was using B.J. Surhoff over there that year and he was probably better in the outfield. I was really looking to use our whole roster and broached it with Cal. When we did get Bordick, Cal was all for [the move] to make us a better team, and Cal was all for us being a better team."

When he got to Baltimore, Bordick still wasn't sure about the situation. He was coming to town to take

MR. RIPKEN, MEET MR. BORDICK

By | Craig Heist

In 1995 he was coming off a season in which he committed just 10 errors. He was a free agent and looking to get a bit closer to home.

"I remember getting a call," Bordick said. "Pat Gillick called my agent and was showing some interest, and I remember saying, 'Yeah, right, that's really going to happen.' I was just pursuing other opportunities. We kept getting calls from Pat, and he basically let it be known [Ripken's move to third base] was going to happen with or without me."

Actually, then Orioles manager Davey Johnson had considered making the move during the 1996 season.

"The year before, I broached it with Cal," Johnson said. "Cal has a lot of pride, and I probably handled that all wrong. I felt no one could play shortstop better, and maybe he had lost a step here and there, but he would make that up by knowing the hitters and playing them well.

over the shortstop position from a hometown hero and living legend.

"As I thought about it, I wanted to make sure everything was all right with Cal," Bordick said. "Cal basically told me that as a professional you have to do what is best for you and your family. When I was out on the West Coast, I wanted to get closer to home, and the East Coast was a good thing."

Nonetheless, the move was not easy for Bordick. In fact, the situation made him very apprehensive.

"It was a little tricky at first," he said. "I obviously had confidence in my abilities at shortstop, but to be standing there next to the best shortstop in the history of the game and coming to Baltimore where he is a living legend was a little overwhelming. What helped my transition was that the whole team was made up of great guys that made me feel good – Chris Hoiles, Jimmy Key and Eric Davis."

– Mr. Ripken, Meet Mr. Bordick –

The 1997 team won 98 games while going wire-to-wire to win the American League East. They beat the Seattle Mariners in four games in the divisional series only to lose the ALCS to the Cleveland Indians in six games.

"That year was a lot of fun and for me personally even with a lot of things going on," Bordick said. "Offensively, I didn't do too much to help the team, but there was such a great cast of players, and we just won. That's what Baltimore wanted, and that's what Pat Gillick wanted. I was glad I could come over and help us get there. We didn't reach our ultimate goal, but I think everybody in our clubhouse and all of Baltimore felt we were the best team in baseball. It just didn't work out in the end."

Bordick and Ripken talked about the transition quite a bit that year. Bordick came to realize later in his career just how hard it was for Ripken to make the move.

"I think the bottom line is, when you play a position your whole life and someone tells you to move, you aren't going to feel good about it," Bordick said. "At the end of my career, all of a sudden they were telling me you are going to be a utility player after I had played shortstop for 10 years. I didn't feel good about it. I totally understand that situation, and all Cal did was

go out and make the All-Star team again, have a great year and become one of the game's best third basemen, so he proved what kind of an amazing athlete and professional he is."

As Bordick settled in at shortstop and played with Ripken over the next four years, he developed an appreciation for Ripken far beyond his role as a baseball player.

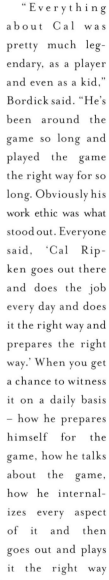

"Everything about Cal was pretty much legendary, as a player and even as a kid," Bordick said. "He's been around the game so long and played the game the right way for so long. Obviously his work ethic was what stood out. Everyone said, 'Cal Ripken goes out there and does the job every day and does it the right way and prepares the right way.' When you get a chance to witness it on a daily basis – how he prepares himself for the game, how he talks about the game, how he internalizes every aspect of it and then goes out and plays it the right way every night for as long as he did, day in and day out — it's amazing.

"Obviously Cal went through a couple of different generations of baseball, and he got into a position where he was a superstar in the game. He was like a mega superstar, where the things he did off the field reflected on him as well, and nobody carried himself better than

– Mr. Ripken, Meet Mr. Bordick –

him. Not only was he the great professional on the field, but off the field he did everything the right way, which nowadays — I'm not going to say it's rare because there are a lot of great people who do the right thing — I don't know if there is anyone who has done it better."

Ripken's ability to do everything the right way was never more evident than when he decided to end the streak on Sept. 20, 1998 at home. Ripken had thought about ending the streak on the final game of the season in Boston, but after discussing it with his wife Kelly, he decided the best way would be to do it at home (against the Yankees) in front of the home fans.

It was a pretty well-kept secret until just minutes before game time.

"Cal and I played catch before every game," Bordick said. "I jumped out there ready to go. I was looking for Cal, and he was sitting on the bench talking to someone. I said, 'Hey Cal, hey Rip, come on,' and he shook his head. Then I got this really weird feeling.

"Cal said, 'I am going out in the bullpen tonight.' That's when my heart kind of sank, and I really had mixed emotions. At first I felt like crying, I really did. I mean, you think about what he felt like and everything he's gone through his whole career. People were on him about being out there during the streak — take a day off, this and that. He persevered through all of that and became one of the greatest shortstops in the history of the game. He is going to be a first-ballot Hall of Famer, and all of a sudden he says 'This is the night I am going to take off.' It must have been gut-wrenching for him to make that decision.

"At first, I felt bad. Then I felt good for him. I felt like, 'Wow, that's incredible, way to go, Cal. That was the most amazing thing that's ever been done in the

history of sports. Tonight's the night you are putting your glove down.' Unbelievable emotion."

Another thing Bordick would learn about Ripken over time was the degree of the Iron Man's toughness.

"He is, mentally, probably tougher than anyone who has ever played," Bordick said. "You have to be to run yourself out there, day in and day out, in pain, knowing you're sore. Incredible mental toughness. When you think of him you have to think of the ultimate whole package. If you could gift wrap the perfect athlete as far as mental toughness and physical ability, Cal is the guy."

To this day, Bordick still can't get over how fortunate he was to have played with Ripken by his side.

"Every time I was around Cal — and I consider Cal my friend, I played with him a long time and I could joke around with him — I always felt like I was in the presence of something incredible," Bordick said. "Like star-struck almost. I had that feeling every day, and I'd watch him take his ground balls and do his business, and he has a great aura about him, and I think everyone around him feels that."

Bordick said he knows Cal got a bad rap from time to time about The Streak, but he knows that even without it, 400 home runs and 3,000 hits makes Ripken a first-ballot Hall of Famer.

"No doubt about it," Bordick said. "The things he did on the field numbers-wise, he could have missed a whole year and still have been put in the Hall of Fame on the first ballot for the things he did. He changed the game at shortstop. Such a big strong guy, playing shortstop with such agility and athleticism and before you know it, that's the way it is now. So many great shortstops have size and strength and power and he brought that to the game." ☐

CRAIG HEIST IS A SPORTS REPORTER FOR WTOP RADIO AND ESPN RADIO AND A FREQUENT CONTRIBUTOR TO PRESSBOX.

> "IF YOU COULD GIFT WRAP THE PERFECT ATHLETE AS FAR AS MENTAL TOUGHNESS AND PHYSICAL ABILITY, CAL IS THE GUY."
>
> – Mike Bordick –

When Cal Ripken played his first game for the Orioles on Aug. 10, 1981, no one could have imagined or predicted the kind of career that was about to unfold.

Ripken's numbers have been well documented: 431 home runs, 3,184 hits, 19 All-Star games, the last of which came in Seattle with a home run and an MVP award.

And, oh yeah, there was that little thing called "the streak."

Ripken tied and broke the record of 2,130 consecutive games held by Lou Gehrig on Sept. 5 and 6, 1995. He went on to play in 501 more consecutive games before finally ending the streak on Sept. 20, 1998, at home against the Yankees.

toothbrush to the counter. We put buckets of water over the door, pine needles in the bed, hid his clothes. We just terrorized him. I remember we put cellophane over the toilet bowl. It was good clean fun."

After a few years in the majors, Dempsey saw a change in Ripken.

"He became more focused and a little more secluded. When the record and the streak started, I think there was a lot of pressure on Cal. I think he realized at that point there were a lot of sacrifices that had to be made, and he was willing to do it. He dug in for the long haul."

What makes the streak impressive, according to Dempsey, was Ripken's mental toughness and approach to the game.

"It's the mind-set," Dempsey said. "It's the physical toughness and a lot of the things he had to overcome

THE TEAMMATES

By | Craig Heist

The highlights of his career are endless and amazing. In fact, for as much as we are in awe of what Cal accomplished, his teammates were even more amazed and honored to be part of it.

Rick Dempsey played with Ripken for the first five seasons of Cal's career, and the former catcher says the first thing he noticed about Ripken was the raw talent of the athlete.

"He could do anything because he had that ability," Dempsey said. "He could play tiddlywinks left-handed and be good at it. He was one of those kids, he was big and strong with a lot of endurance, and he was smart. You knew he was going to figure it out."

Dempsey roomed for a time with Ripken, and he said there was a side of Cal not many people knew about, the mischievous side.

"Oh, he did anything," Dempsey said. "We pulled a lot of pranks together. We had a broadcaster, Tom Marr; we called him two-ton Tommy Marr. We used to just terrorize him. We would pick the locks on his room and glue his

to get there. There were a lot of times where I am sure he didn't feel like playing. I know there were a couple of years where the batting average wasn't as high as he expected, so he may have wanted to put it all behind him because it became frustrating. He was one of those people who couldn't be out of the lineup and not because of the streak. He just didn't want the game to start without him."

Outfielder Mike Devereaux came to the Orioles after playing with the Dodgers. He played with the O's from 1989 to 1994 and when he got here the streak was in high gear.

"When I was first got to Baltimore, I remember saying to myself, 'Man, Cal has played all these consecutive games in a row,' and then I started to calculate it," Devereaux said. "I calculated for Cal to break the record he would have to play another seven years. Knowing the rules of baseball like I did, I knew after six years I was going to be a free agent, and then I thought, 'Man, I'm not going to be around when Cal breaks the record.'"

– The Teammates –

He was right. Devereaux was gone in 1995 but returned to the club for the wild-card year of 1996. To this day, he is still amazed Ripken was able to play every single day for as long as he did.

"To be honest, I don't know how he did it," Devereaux said. "He had a way of controlling himself. He had a way of protecting himself where he didn't get hurt, and I always didn't like the criticism of people saying he should sit down.

"It's an incredible thing, and I am definitely honored to have played with Cal, who is one of the most respected players to ever play the game."

There were a few times during Ripken's career in which the streak could have come to an end. One of those times occurred on June 6, 1993, during the famous brawl between the Orioles and the Seattle Mariners.

Oriole pitcher Mike Mussina hit Mariners catcher Bill Hasselman with a pitch, the benches emptied, and Ripken twisted his right knee in the bottom of the pile. Mussina remembers that day but didn't know until later how badly Ripken was hurt. In fact, if the Orioles had a game the next day, Ripken probably wouldn't have been able to play.

"It wasn't until I saw a replay that specifically had him in the play that I realized something happened to him," Mussina said. "Of course he never tells you how bad he is. He played later in his career with a bad back, and you never really knew how bad it was until he couldn't physically stand anymore, so that was just another example."

Mussina played a very big role the night Ripken broke Gehrig's record. He was the starting pitcher against the Angels.

"It was pretty exciting," he said. "By then I had been playing a little while. It was an honor to have my day to pitch come on that day. In the first inning I gave up a solo homer and there was all this celebration going on and I go out and give one up, and I remember telling myself I better get my head in the game because the last thing we want is to lose the day he breaks this record."

Mussina didn't lose on that night, thanks in great part to Ripken. Not only did Ripken homer in the record-tying game the night before, but he also took Shawn Boskie deep in the record-breaking game as well.

"I just thought it was unique and amazing he would do it those two days in a row," Mussina said. "He had a way of pulling things off like that."

It was Ripken's steadiness and consistency that Mussina will remember the most about his teammate.

"Just having him out there every day was big," Mussina said. "Every time I went out there to pitch, I knew he was going to be out there playing shortstop. I knew he was the smartest player on the field and understood everything about the game and what I was trying to do. It just takes one little small thing out of your mind."

Rafael Palmeiro, who joined the Orioles in 1994, saw many of the same things on the field Mussina saw.

"He was the quarterback," Palmeiro said. "There were times when he was out there and I don't know if he ever called pitches and things like that. I know he was criticized for things like that at times, but he was really smart. He knew the game inside and out. He knew the opponent. He

– The Teammates –

knew baseball as well as anyone I have ever known and he understood it and prepared for it, and I think that's why he had the type of career he had He was ready every day."

Palmeiro remembers those two nights in September 1995 as a celebration — from the fans' enthusiasm, to the home runs, and then, on the record-breaking night, he and Bobby Bonilla pushing Cal out of the dugout to take a curtain-call lap around the stadium.

"Those two nights were incredible," Palmeiro said. "It was his time. It was all about him and not about anyone else. It was not about our team or about us winning or losing; it was about a baseball celebration. He had done something that had only been done once before in the history of the game. This was a baseball celebration that was being celebrated all around the country.

"When we pushed him out [of the dugout], he didn't want any part of it. He just wanted to tip his cap and continue on because he was all about just playing the game; let's get the win and go home. But this was about a career achievement that deserved its moment, and he didn't want it.

"You know what we said: 'You are going to go out there and you are going to soak it in. This is your moment, you've earned it, you have a right and everyone wants to see you.' He did, and I think now it's become something that people think back on and see him running around and appreciating the fans."

Ripken touched almost everyone he played with throughout his career. From guys like Dempsey, Mussina and Palmeiro, to younger guys like Orioles second baseman Brian Roberts, who was starting his Oriole career when Ripken was ending his in 2001.

Ripken was always teaching. He was a manager on the field, and he had no trouble passing his knowledge of the game on to players like Roberts.

"Anytime you get a chance to play with one of the

best players in the game, it's an honor and a privilege," Roberts said. "Growing up and watching him on TV and being a shortstop myself, it was something I never dreamed of — playing beside him, playing next to him on the same team, anything like that. Cal is just a great person to be around and loves the game so much that you can't help but take a lot of stuff away from him.

"As a shortstop, he did everything so fundamentally sound that it was easy for me to watch and to learn from. I was never the flashy type, so for me learning from Cal that way, I really enjoyed watching him."

Orioles shortstop Miguel Tejada currently has the longest consecutive-game streak of any active player in baseball with 1,080 straight games, the seventh longest streak of all time. Now Tejada is getting the Ripken comparisons.

"I was impressed to watch him play because he's the kind of guy that played baseball every day, played for so many years and never had a problem," Tejada said. "You know, he's been unbelievable. I'm proud to play the same position on the same team that he played for. I know it's hard to do what he did so I try to do my best. To be playing every day, to be in the field every day without an injury, it's great."

When there is talk about Cal Ripken, the one word that comes up most often is respect — the respect Ripken had for the game and the respect players who played with and against him had for him.

Maybe former Orioles manager Mike Hargrove spoke for all of Ripken's managers and teammates when asked what it was like to have Cal on his team.

Hargrove paused a moment, then said, "Well, I never had to worry about him."

And neither did we. □

"EVERY TIME I WENT OUT THERE TO PITCH, I KNEW HE WAS GOING TO BE OUT THERE PLAYING SHORTSTOP."

– Mike Mussina –

CRAIG HEIST IS A SPORTS REPORTER FOR WTOP RADIO AND ESPN RADIO AND A FREQUENT CONTRIBUTOR TO PRESSBOX.

GREAT LINEUP CARD CAPER

By | Mike Lurie

Phil Regan's tenure as manager of the Baltimore Orioles was short and not all that sweet.

Say what you will about the savvy the manager lacked in running the 1995 club on the field. As someone with an eye for an historic moment, and the future value of a collectible, Regan had a keen understanding of things.

On Sept. 6, 1995, Regan wrote Cal Ripken Jr.'s name on the lineup card for Ripken's 2,131st consecutive game, the game that would break Lou Gehrig's consecutive-games streak. On an ordinary day, a manager would make two copies of the lineup card. But as millions around the country knew, this was no ordinary day.

So Regan made five copies. He kept one for himself. Three years after the historic night, Regan attempted to auction off the card through a Chicago auction house, along with the pen he used to fill it out.

Price in question? About $40,000. By today's memorabilia standards, just 12 years after the night the streak was broken, it seems like a relative bargain. After the Orioles learned of Regan's attempt to sell the property, the *Baltimore Sun* reported that the Orioles attempted to claim the two items as theirs.

Ultimately, an out-of-court settlement was reached. The *Sun* reported that a Virginia man named Warren Fitzgibbon, then 38, a financial analyst with a government agency in Washington, D.C., paid more than $40,000

for various wares: a copy of the 2,131 card, a copy of the 2,130 card from the record-tying game the previous night, and other memorabilia.

Those developments struck a chord of curiosity with Baltimore attorney David N. Pessin, a partner with the law firm of Hodes, Ulman, Pessin & Katz, P.A., who has specialized in estate planning and elder law, and represented athletes in Major League Baseball, the NFL, NBA and NHL.

Pessin, a former Division I tennis teammate of John Lucas at Maryland in the 1970s, said that he marvels at the leap of faith Regan presumed in holding on to the 2,131 lineup card for future sale.

"I can't think of a single principle of law that would support Phil Regan's contention that he is entitled to that lineup card or any sale of the proceeds of the lineup card," Pessin said.

"In employment law, there's just no single property that would entitle Regan to take and sell the lineup card," Pessin said, "no more so than he could walk into the locker room and walk away with the uniforms. Whether the item in question belongs to the team or to the league, it certainly doesn't belong to the participants."

For the record, the four other copies of the historic lineup card reportedly ended up in various locales. The plate umpire for the game donated his to Bowling Green State University. Another went to the Babe Ruth Museum. Then-California Angels manager Marcel Lachemann reportedly gave his away. The final copy went to Ripken.

Regan isn't alone when it comes to a participant's

> "I CAN'T THINK OF A SINGLE PRINCIPLE OF LAW THAT WOULD SUPPORT PHIL REGAN'S CONTENTION."
>
> – David N. Pessin –

– Great Lineup Card Caper –

view of holding onto baseball history. Nine years after Ripken eclipsed Gehrig's record, the Boston Red Sox ended a streak that was far longer in the making: an 86-year World Series championship drought.

When then-first baseman Doug Mientkiewicz recorded the final out of the 2004 World Series, taking a short toss from closing pitcher Keith Foulke, he held onto the ball for months before the Red Sox asked for its return. A reported agreement was reached early in the 2006 season that sent the ball to its final destination at the Baseball Hall of Fame.

In the Regan case, Pessin suspects that the relatively low price generated for the 2,131 lineup card had another effect: "Maybe we would have seen more action on this if the amount of money in controversy had been more substantial."

There are decent odds that the lineup card would fetch a higher price today.

"But let's be truthful," Pessin adds. "Establishing value for this stuff is so mysterious. Which is more valuable, the one that breaks Ruth's record or the one that breaks Maris' record? And to a certain extent in these cases, you're dealing with living legends, and there can be an almost interminable supply (of certain memorabilia). So the normal laws of supply and demand don't work." □

A LONGTIME SPORTS WRITER FOR NEWSPAPERS AND THE WEB, MIKE LURIE IS CURRENTLY A SPORTS REPORTER ON WYPR RADIO AND WORKS IN INSTITUTIONAL ADVANCEMENT AT UMBC.

THE STARTING LINEUPS

MAY 30, 1982
GAME #1 OF "THE STREAK"
Toronto Blue Jays 6, Baltimore Orioles 0 (at Memorial Stadium)

Blue Jays			Orioles		
1. Damaso Garcia	2B		1. Al Bumbry	CF	
2. Rance Mulliniks	3B		2. Rich Dauer	2B	
3. Willie Upshaw	1B		3. John Lowenstein	LF	
4. Dave Revering	DH		4. Ken Singleton	DH	
5. Barry Bonnell	LF		5. Terry Crowley	1B	
6. Hosken Powell	RF		6. Dan Ford	RF	
7. Ernie Whitt	C		7. Rick Dempsey	C	
8. Lloyd Moseby	CF		8. Cal Ripken	3B	
9. Alfredo Griffin	SS		9. Lenn Sakata	SS	
Jim Gott	P		Jim Palmer	P	

Ripken's Line: 0-2, 1 BB, 1 K

SEPTEMBER 6, 1995
GAME #2131 (RECORD GAME) OF "THE STREAK"
Baltimore Orioles 4, California Angels 2 (at Camden Yards)

Angels			Orioles		
1. Tony Phillips	3B		1. Brady Anderson	CF	
2. Jim Edmonds	CF		2. Manny Alexander	2B	
3. Tim Salmon	RF		3. Rafael Palmeiro	1B	
4. Chili Davis	DH		4. Bobby Bonilla	RF	
5. J.T. Snow	1B		5. Cal Ripken	SS	
6. Garret Anderson	LF		6. Harold Baines	DH	
7. Rex Hudler	2B		7. Chris Hoiles	C	
8. Jorge Fabregas	C		8. Jeff Huson	3B	
9. Damion Easley	SS		9. Mark Smith	LF	
Shawn Boskie	P		Mike Mussina	P	

Ripken's Line: 2-4, HR, RBI, R

SEPTEMBER 5, 1995
GAME #2130 (TYING GAME) OF "THE STREAK"
Baltimore Orioles 8, California Angels 0 (at Camden Yards)

Angels			Orioles		
1. Tony Phillips	3B		1. Brady Anderson	CF	
2. Jim Edmonds	CF		2. Manny Alexander	2B	
3. Tim Salmon	RF		3. Cal Ripken	SS	
4. Chili Davis	DH		4. Bobby Bonilla	RF	
5. J.T. Snow	1B		5. Rafael Palmeiro	1B	
6. Mike Aldrete	LF		6. Chris Hoiles	C	
7. Spike Owen	2B		7. Harold Baines	DH	
8. Greg Myers	C		8. Jeff Manto	3B	
9. Damion Easley	SS		9. Mark Smith	LF	
Brian Anderson	P		Scott Erickson	P	

Ripken's Line: 3-5, HR, RBI, 2 R

SEPTEMBER 20, 1998
FIRST GAME AFTER "THE STREAK"
New York Yankees 5, Baltimore Orioles 4 (at Camden Yards)

Yankees			Orioles		
1. Chuck Knoblauch	2B		1. Roberto Alomar	2B	
2. Derek Jeter	SS		2. Brady Anderson	CF	
3. Bernie Williams	CF		3. Willie Greene	RF	
4. Chili Davis	DH		4. Rafael Palmeiro	1B	
5. Jorge Posada	C		5. Calvin Pickering	DH	
6. Tim Raines	LF		6. Ryan Minor	3B	
7. Chad Curtis	RF		7. B.J. Surhoff	LF	
8. Mike Lowell	3B		8. Lenny Webster	C	
9. Luis Sojo	1B		9. Mike Bordick	SS	
Orlando Hernandez	P		Doug Johns	P	

THE PLAY'S THE THING

By | Stan "The Fan" Charles

Plenty of people can write about Cal Ripken Jr. I can write about Cal as I laid witness to him back in the day, and I don't exactly speak from a place others do. As Stan "The Fan," Baltimore's preeminent Orioles sports talker during all of Cal's career, I can honestly say that I talked about Cal Ripken and The Streak more than any other human being on the planet.

Sometimes I was right, a lot of times I was wrong, but regardless of my score, Baltimoreans loved — and still love — to talk about Ripken: what made him tick, what made him go on and on like the Energizer bunny.

More times than not, the subjects fans talked about most were streak-related and whether Cal should continue toward Lou Gehrig's record. Some said Cal should sit, that he wasn't helping the team. A handful of fans thought Cal should take a day off here and there, that he would be better off for it. Most knew that if this was anyone else, without this streak, the manager would sit Cal down.

On and on this went, week after week, month after month, All-Star break after All-Star break. The talk was there when Earl Weaver managed the team the second time around in 1985-86. Talk of the streak began to bubble during the 1987 season, when Cal Sr. managed the Birds, and it never truly died until Ray Miller, at Cal's request, wrote out a lineup card near the end of the 1998 season that didn't have No. 8 penciled in its regular spot.

By this time I had long since ceased to care much about the discussion of whether the streak was good or bad for the Orioles and for Cal. He had broken Gehrig's consecutive-game streak in 1995, and he broke Sachio Kimugasa's world mark of 2,215 in June 1997.

But I certainly never got bored of talking about what made Cal tick — mostly because of one play in the hot summer of 1993, when I realized that while Cal may have wanted the streak to continue, he was not going to let The Streak define how he played the game.

What made the nights of Sept. 5 and 6, 1995 so special was how many of the nights building up to Cal's 2,131st consecutive game were just baseball games.

Nothing special seemed to happen night after night as 500 consecutive games turned into 925 consecutive games, and then 1,375, and then 1,750. The sheer inertia of the streak took on an inevitability that defied logic.

And so it was with that backdrop that the game at Camden Yards on June 9, 1993 began. The Orioles took the field on that day with Rick Sutcliffe pitching for the O's against Bob Welch of the Oakland A's. After Sutcliffe retired the A's routinely in the top of the first, the Orioles came to the plate against Welch.

Brady Anderson led off and hit into the first out of the inning. Mark McLemore was up next and he singled to center. With one on and one out, Ripken was hit high on his left shoulder by a Welch fastball, an early and

I REALIZED CAL WAS UNAFRAID OF INJURY ... AND SIMPLY PLAYED THE GAME AS HARD AS HE HAD TO AT ANY GIVEN TIME.

– The Play's The Thing –

intimidating wake-up call. I remember how uncharacteristically upset Cal was about this obvious attempt to brush him back. Hit by the pitch, Cal jumped up and began to trot down to first, jawing some un-Cal like remarks Welch's way.

Recently, a Cal confidant and I talked about the play. He told me what had angered Cal so much. As Cal rose from the ground after being hit by Welch, Cal asked A's catcher Terry Steinbach if the brush-back had been intentional. Steinbach responded with a sarcastic, "No, we would never do that."

As Cal jogged to first, lashing out at Welch, he made up his mind if given the opportunity he would take out the A's shortstop. Ironically, that shortstop was Mike Bordick, the player who eventually would come to Baltimore as

the key component in Cal's move to third for the 1997 season.

As the inning developed, McLemore, who had reached base earlier in the inning, and Ripken moved up to third and second, respectively, on a groundout to third by Harold Baines. No revenge was possible on Bordick.

Next up was Mike Devereaux, who lashed a hard line single to right. As Cal took off, I remembered how angry he had been after being hit by the high hard one thrown

by Welch.

As Cal rounded third, I sensed that a message was about to be sent. The play was not a normal bang-bang play, because catcher Steinbach clearly had the ball, which allowed Cal a clean shot at knocking the ball loose. But Cal's agenda went beyond knocking the ball loose, and Steinbach just happened to be the wrong guy at the wrong place.

The collision was violent. The ball did not come loose from Steinbach's grasp, and the inning ended. Steinbach was out for the game, and I learned a lot about Cal watching that half-inning. I realized Cal was unafraid of injury, and the by-product of the streak ending, and simply played the game as hard as he had to at any given time.

I can't say for sure that nobody ever threw at Cal again. But I know this: much like Ishmael, the narrator in "Moby Dick", told us the horror of the insane quest for the white whale, Steinbach, Welch, the Oakland A's and anyone who saw that one play passed the word throughout MLB that it was not a smart thing to anger Cal Ripken. ☐

A VETERAN OF MORE THAN 20 YEARS OF SPORTS TALK RADIO IN BALTIMORE, STAN "THE FAN" CHARLES IS CURRENTLY THE PUBLISHER OF PRESSBOX.

e knew early on Cal Ripken Jr. would be a special player. What we didn't know was how much he would have a flair for the dramatic.

Not flashy or a showman, this workmanlike Hall of Famer had a sense of theater that flourished under the glare of history's spotlight.

There were the home runs, of course, on those two incredible nights at Camden Yards when he tied and broke Lou Gehrig's record, the second of which was punctuated by a 22-minute lap around the field.

I covered Ripken for more than eight years and will never forget those nights, but the needle of my No. 8 memory meter also jumps when I think of his final All-Star Game, a magical night of drama in Seattle.

Jeter and Nomar Garciaparra were the others – motioned Ripken to switch places.

Ripken didn't know what to do, but AL manager Joe Torre stood on the top step of the dugout and motioned him to do it.

A roar from the crowd grew when it realized it was witnessing one of those spontaneous moments that make sports so great.

Only it wasn't spontaneous.

As I learned when covering Rodriguez in New York, this is a player sensitive to the game's history. He is one who appreciates the unique drama of the sport.

On the Thursday prior to the game, Rodriguez, then with the Seattle Mariners, phoned Torre and bounced the idea.

A SECRET IN SEATTLE

By | John Delcos

Ripken was playing third base then, and moments before the first pitch American League shortstop Alex Rodriguez motioned him to switch positions, thereby giving him one last start at shortstop.

Of course, Ripken later hit a home run.

Derek Jeter later remarked that Ripken always seemed to hit a home run in the games in which he was spotlighted, and it was true.

The position switch caught everybody, even Ripken, by surprise.

Ripken, of course, received a huge ovation in the pregame introductions, and moments later the American League took the field. Ripken played 12 All-Star Games at shortstop, and wouldn't it be nice for him to play there in his final one?

Ripken spoke of it the day before and numerous journalists in the press box were chatting up the idea.

"Oh my god, he's going to short," I said to somebody sitting next to me.

Just before the first pitch, Rodriguez, one of the then-Three Amigos as Ripken's heir apparent to the position –

"I thought it was a dynamite idea," said Torre, who let most of the team in on what would happen.

"The only one we tried to keep out of it was Cal," Torre said. "If we did, he wouldn't do it."

Rodriguez was insistent. He and Ripken had become close, and the future Hall of Famer counseled the other future Hall of Famer on the trappings of stardom.

It was Rodriguez's way of saying thank you.

"It was an opportunity to let everybody reminisce about what a great career he had as a shortstop," Rodriguez said.

Ripken was touched.

"It was a really neat tribute," Ripken said that night. "I spent most of my career out at shortstop. It was great being at shortstop again. I appreciated it."

Years later, when Rodriguez was making the transition to third base in spring training, Ripken counseled him again, perhaps returning the favor.

"Cal has always been great to me," Rodriguez said that spring with the Yankees when he moved to third base. "He's so unselfish. That's what made him the player he was. He's one of a kind."

– A Secret In Seattle –

And one with flair, and it flashed two innings later.

Ripken received another standing ovation in the third inning when he stepped up to the plate against Chan Ho Park.

As Ripken stepped out of the batter's box, it was obvious what people were thinking.

"The ovation, with people standing up, I came out and tried to acknowledge them very quickly because I don't want the game to be delayed for that," Ripken said. "I got back in and just saw the first pitch, swung at it and put a nice swing on it."

There are few sounds in sports so distinguishable as bat meeting ball squarely.

Torre was thinking about what lineup changes to make when the crack returned him to the field.

"It was really magical," Torre said. "And Cal is such a class individual. His legacy in baseball is not going to be how he played, but the way he played, the way he carried himself and it was wonderful." □

JOHN DELCOS COVERED CAL RIPKEN AND THE ORIOLES FROM 1990–98 WITH THE YORK DAILY RECORD. HE CURRENTLY COVERS THE METS FOR GANNETT NEWSPAPERS IN WESTCHESTER, N.Y.

CAL RIPKEN CAREER ALL-STAR GAME STATISTICS

Year	Team	G	AB	R	H	2B	3B	HR	RBI	BB	SO	SB	OBP	SLG	AVG
1983	AL	1	0	0	0	0	0	0	0	1	0	0	1.000	-	-
1984	AL	1	3	0	0	0	0	0	0	0	0	0	.000	.000	.000
1985	AL	1	3	0	1	0	0	0	0	0	0	0	.333	.333	.333
1986	AL	1	4	0	0	0	0	0	0	0	2	0	.000	.000	.000
1987	AL	1	2	0	1	0	0	0	0	0	0	0	.500	.500	.500
1988	AL	1	3	0	0	0	0	0	0	1	0	0	.250	.000	.000
1989	AL	1	3	0	1	1	0	0	0	0	0	0	.333	.667	.333
1990	AL	1	2	0	0	0	0	0	0	0	0	0	.000	.000	.000
1991	AL	1	3	1	2	0	0	1	3	0	0	0	.667	1.667	.667
1992	AL	1	3	0	1	0	0	0	1	0	0	0	.333	.333	.333
1993	AL	1	3	0	0	0	0	0	0	0	1	0	.000	.000	.000
1994	AL	1	5	0	1	1	0	0	0	0	2	0	.200	.400	.200
1995	AL	1	3	0	2	0	0	0	0	0	0	0	.667	.667	.667
1996	AL	1	3	0	0	0	0	0	0	0	0	0	.000	.000	.000
1997	AL	1	2	0	1	0	0	0	0	0	0	0	.500	.500	.500
1998	AL	1	4	1	1	1	0	0	2	0	0	0	.250	.500	.250
1999	AL	1	1	1	1	0	0	0	1	0	0	0	1.000	1.000	1.000
2001	AL	1	2	1	1	0	0	1	1	0	0	0	.500	2.000	.500
Totals:		18	49	4	13	3	0	2	8	2	5	0	.308	.499	.265

⊢ * CAL WAS ALSO SELECTED TO THE AMERICAN LEAGUE ALL-STAR TEAM IN 2000, BUT DID NOT PLAY. ⊣

THE PERSONAL SIDE

By | Chris Berman

The night that Cal Ripken Jr. broke Lou Gehrig's consecutive-game streak was not only a great night for Cal, and a great night for baseball, it was a great night for America.

Cal epitomizes the work ethic of packing a lunch, going to work, doing your job no matter how you feel, and coming home. Obviously, the pay level and the publicity are different playing shortstop for the Orioles compared to working in an auto factory, but I still believe the basic work ethic that America was built on was exemplified by Cal Ripken that night.

Joe DiMaggio was there, which was unbelievable. President Clinton was there, which was unbelievable. The Oriole family — Earl Weaver, Brooks Robinson, Cal's dad, right on down the line — was there. It was great.

It's a night none of us will ever forget. Because as much as you never know when entering the ball park if you'll hit four home runs or pitch a no-hitter, in this case Cal knew he was going to the park and was going to surpass Lou Gehrig's record. Still, it was spontaneous — what he did with the fans, the great feeling in the crowd. There were more people crying — including Buck Martinez and I in the ESPN booth — than I'd ever seen before at a non-funeral, at a happy event. We were quiet for more than 20 minutes, and we were probably crying for 10 of them.

Professionally, I have been at ESPN for 27 years, and this was the highlight of my career. Buck and I thank Cal for letting us be part of it. We were just smart enough to get out of the way and let America see what we were seeing.

I'll never forget it — the home run, the home run the night before. Actually, the home run the night before was more daunting — when 2,130 went up, when he tied Gehrig. That was, "Wow, that's heavy."

As for individual accomplishments, what Cal Ripken did is one of the most impressive in any sport at any time. □

A SIX-TIME NATIONAL SPORTSCASTER OF THE YEAR FOR ESPN, CHRIS BERMAN SERVES AS NFL STUDIO HOST, SPORTSCENTER ANCHOR AND BASEBALL COMMENTATOR. BERMAN CALLED ESPN'S EMMY-AWARD WINNING TELECAST OF CAL RIPKEN'S 2,131ST CONSECUTIVE GAME SEPT. 6, 1995.

By | Bill Stetka

I am a few years older than Cal, but I think we've always had something of a kinship because of our shared Harford County roots. I've gone through three professional phases with him: as a reporter, covering Cal in his early years with the Orioles; as an official scorer, responsible for helping extend (or end) some of the records he set; and as part of the Orioles public relations staff as he broke Lou Gehrig's record, ended his own streak and eventually retired.

Certainly, what happened the nights of Sept. 5 and 6, 1995, stands out and is the thing I'm asked most about. I'm proud to have played a small part. But my most vivid recollections of Cal have nothing to do with things that happened on the field. It wasn't until I went to work for the Orioles in the public relations department that I truly got a grasp of Cal, the person.

Fans heard a lot about how Cal played for The Streak, and how he nurtured the record. Anyone who watched as he wrestled with teammates or the clubhouse kids before games, falling over couches, taking and giving punches, knows that isn't true. While the streak was something Cal was obviously proud of, being part of the clubhouse camaraderie was just as important to him. That went on until very late in his career, when back pain finally sidelined him and the Orioles' clubhouse as a whole took on a different character.

– The Personal Side –

That is one side of Cal that, especially during the "streak years," few people took note of. Anyone playing just for the streak would not have exposed himself to the potential for injuries that Cal did off the field. Wasn't it tough enough playing shortstop through all of that?

And almost every day, after exchanging punches to the ribs or wrestling a teammate to the floor, Cal would pick himself up, put on his jersey and head off to tend to something many of us found even more daunting.

The time Cal spent with children and adults who were facing a trauma or terminal illness was unbelievable to all of us who watched it. From the time I started working in the PR department in 1995 until the day he retired seven seasons later, there was hardly a day that went by when Cal did not meet with someone — a 10-year-old with cancer, a 40-year-old awaiting a new heart, or a 60-year-old with ALS — sometimes on the field, but more often away from the media and the public, in the video room off the Orioles' clubhouse.

And these were not just a fly-by, say-hello-and-sign-an-autograph meet-and-greet. He would engage the patients and their families in conversation, asking them questions about anything from where they were from to their favorite subject in school — and then relate stories that connected him to their hometown, or to his own homework problems. For the next 15 or 20 minutes, the game about to take place on the field was not as important to him as these people were.

By meeting with them, talking with them, he eased their trauma and gave them something good to remember. This happened night after night, and watching his ability to make each visit special — to make each person he met feel comfortable and important, no matter their personal pain — was more amazing than seeing him play 2,362 consecutive games. I am not the only person who felt the need to leave the room and regain my composure on more than a few occasions.

Many players are just as giving and generous of their time, but I'm not sure any have done it with the spotlight glaring on them the way it did on Cal. And when I think of him, it is those times and those moments that leave me more in awe than anything he did on the field. ☐

BILL STETKA IS CURRENTLY THE DIRECTOR OF MEDIA RELATIONS AND PUBLICATIONS FOR THE ORIOLES. HE SERVED AS THE TEAM'S DIRECTOR OF PUBLIC RELATIONS FROM 1999 TO 2003 AND ASSISTANT DIRECTOR OF PUBLIC RELATIONS FROM 1995 TO 1999.

By | John Maroon

I first met Cal Ripken on a flight from Baltimore to Florida after the 1994-1995 work stoppage was settled. I got the job as the Orioles' director of public relations between the end of the strike-shortened 1994 season and the start of the 1995 campaign. We met briefly on the flight and decided we would get together after the first workout the following day to talk about what would be the most media-crazed year of his Hall of Fame career.

1995 was the year Cal would break the thought-to-be-unbreakable record for consecutive games played, held by the legendary Lou Gehrig. It was no secret that the demands on Cal that season would be tremendous from the fans and the media. And oh yeah, he would actually have to play baseball as well.

When we got together during spring training, Cal was clear that he wanted to try to make everyone happy, but he didn't want this to be a distraction to teammates. As I thought this through I made a suggestion: how about you meet with the media the first day in every city to discuss the streak, but we would ask the media to make that the only time the streak was discussed during the series.

Cal was skeptical (he always is) but was willing to give it a try. He asked that we conduct the meeting with the media very early before his teammates arrive so it would not be a burden to them. With the help of my fellow PR people around the league, we made it work and work well. Cal enjoyed the process and media members got everything they needed.

As a result of this and a year of closely working together during an international media crush, Cal and I formed a very close professional and personal relationship, a relationship that I, to this day, value a great deal.

Cal and I seem to be on the same page when it comes to working with the media and we share a similar sense of humor. He is one of the most thoughtful and genuine people I have had the honor of knowing and I am as excited as anyone for him, Kelly and the kids about his election to the Hall of Fame.

The way Cal has represented the game of baseball is, in my mind, the way all athletes should represent their sports.

– The Personal Side –

He works hard at his craft while understanding that there are other things that need to be considered. Most notably, the fans and the media. Cal always understood his responsibilities beyond playing and he had a desire to treat all the aspects of his career with class and dignity.

I am very fortunate I worked with Cal during his playing career. I work closely with him and serve as his spokesman. I have seen him continue to grow and evolve in this new phase of his life as a businessman and a philanthropist.

His passion for his business, as well as his desire to make sure that the foundation named for his father makes a real impact, is impressive and admirable.

Sometimes a guy just has it all. He is a smart, thoughtful, caring person with a wonderful wife and two great kids. Cal has earned everything that he has, especially the honor that will be bestowed on him in July. □

JOHN MAROON SERVED AS PUBLIC RELATIONS DIRECTOR FOR THE ORIOLES FROM 1995 TO 1999. FROM 2000 TO 2006, HE OVERSAW ALL COMMUNICATIONS FOR RIPKEN BASEBALL AND ITS SUBSIDIARIES AND SERVED AS THE SPOKESPERSON FOR RIPKEN BASEBALL AND CAL RIPKEN JR. HE IS CURRENTLY THE PRESIDENT OF MAROON PR.

By | Dr. Charles A. Steinberg

hat a privilege it is to flip through memries of working with Cal Ripken Jr. and to explore illustrative anecdotes.

As I think of all of his achievements, the one for which I most respect him — and there are so many from which to choose — is the way he honored the values of The Oriole Way and maintained a tradition that could have fallen by the wayside.

I fell in love with baseball on Oct. 9, 1966, shortly after Paul Blair's catch and Brooks Robinson's famous leap that signified Baltimore's first-ever World Championship. Would you believe four straight?

But at age 7, I had ignored the fabulous season. It was only after the Game 4 win, when my mother of blessed memory took my sister and me downtown. She anticipated a spontaneous civic celebration of festivity and joy. We parked near the Lord Baltimore Hotel. Horns were blowing, streamers were flying, people were hugging. A big kid, about 14, told me to get the autograph of a man getting into a taxicab: Alvin Dark. He then pointed to another: Harry Walker. Each signed my brand new flannel 1966 World Champions banner. I loved the city's reaction to the action that had taken place on the field.

More than 25 years later, after so many unfathomable dreams had come true, I shared that story with my friend and colleague. Cal smiled and said, "Same day."

Six-year-old Cal had actually attended that clinching game — afforded tickets because his dad, also of blessed memory, worked for the organization.

When Frank Robinson's home run thrilled the sold-out crowd as the only run of the game, the 6-year-old knew what he wanted to be: not only a baseball player, but an Oriole.

We both fell in love with the Orioles the same day — and he went on to honor that love in a way that paid homage to the organization and to the man who personified its heroes — Brooks Robinson. Who doesn't have a print of Norman Rockwell's perfect painting, "Gee, Thanks Brooks"?

And each of us who grew up in the perfect time to be an Orioles fan met Brooks, felt his warmth, saw his smile, and received his autograph. For many of us, many times over. That made us love him even more as he saved game after game.

Cal not only reminded us of Brooks, he set out to honor his hero with his own behavior and heroism. Cal understood how important it was to be kind to fans, especially children. Brooks had taught that to a generation of Orioles fans.

One day, during spring training at Sarasota, Fla., Cal asked me to walk with him from the clubhouse to the area where fans were crowded to get autographs as players walked along a path. A snow fence separated fans from players.

Cal wanted me to see the scene as he saw it. It worried him. As I stood alongside him and looked into the faces from his point of view, I saw the problem. The push and crush of fans five or six feet tall was painting expressions of anxiety, fear and despair on the faces of precious pint-sized children no more than three or four feet tall. The children were up front, but adults couldn't see how they were getting squeezed against the fence. What should have been a perfect Norman Rockwell scene was frightening and sad. It was the scene that only Cal could see, and he knew that we must find a way to preserve the intimacy of the meeting without the threat of injury to the very children we used to be.

He invented a better way. Years later, long after I left a club in metamorphosis and headed to San Diego, Cal was making his farewell visit to Anaheim. A single-file, orderly line descended down the aisle. The fan at the bottom was the "on deck" fan. On cue, this fan would take several magical steps across to the next aisle, where Cal waited with his blue-eyed smile, just like

– The Personal Side –

Brooks'. The fans had private, personal moments with their hero — an Oriole who emulated Brooks, who celebrated Elrod Hendricks, who contributed to the community as Jim Palmer did, who played every day as Eddie Murray did, and who, in 1995, saved not game after game, but the game itself.

Rockwell would have loved it.

To those of us who did see it, day after day, year after year, we know that Cal understood a phenomenon unique to Baltimore: the love of a hero who loves you back.

That's why, when we created the ceremonies to close Memorial Stadium, Brooks Robinson was the first player to take his position, and, after all the others had made their memorable trots, Cal would be the last.

Brooks to Cal — a span from 1955 to 2001 — was a part of history during which all of us learned the sweetest part of being an Orioles fan. The love affair was real. The players cared about the fans as much as the fans cared about the players. The organization completed the triangle with its care of the players and the fans. Heart and sentiment, loyalty and kindness, doing things right and treating people well — that was the magic of Orioles' baseball.

For perpetuating that class in the manner of Brooks Robinson, we say, "Gee, Thanks Cal." ☐

DR. CHARLES A. STEINBERG SERVED AS DIRECTOR OF PUBLIC AF-FAIRS FOR THE ORIOLES FROM 1992 TO 1995. HE WAS ALSO THE DI-RECTOR OF ORIOLE PRODUCTIONS FROM 1982 TO 1991. HE IS CUR-RENTLY THE EXECUTIVE VICE PRESIDENT OF PUBLIC AFFAIRS FOR THE BOSTON RED SOX.

By | Richard Vaughn

I was hired by the Orioles as assistant public relations director in November of 1984. A few short weeks into my new job, someone came to our office and said a few of the players were over in the clubhouse, Cal Ripken Jr. among them.

It was December, and in the concrete bowels of Memorial Stadium it was cold, really cold. I wasn't sure what they were doing in the clubhouse in December, but I was anxious to meet all of the players, especially Cal, and didn't want to pass up the opportunity.

I made my way over from my tiny cubicle in the public relations office to the Orioles clubhouse. Like I said, it was cold and I was a little nervous. Here I was — two weeks on the job, a rookie — getting ready to open the door of the famed Orioles clubhouse and meet the 1983 American League Most Valuable Player.

I put my hand on the knob and turned. It was unlocked but it wouldn't open. It seemed to be stuck. I pushed and pushed and finally budged it a little. I managed to stick my head in and looked around and couldn't figure out what I was seeing. I saw Cal flying by, then what looked like his brother, Bill ... then Jim Traber and another player — who I later learned was John Habyan — dashing all over the clubhouse. What the hell was going on?

What was going on...was hockey...or some derivation of it. The four teammates were playing two-on-two on the tile floor, using a baseball and bats for a puck and sticks. They had put benches down along the walls to serve as side boards (the reason I couldn't open the door).

As I would come to find out numerous times over the next 10 years, if Cal was involved in playing something, anything, there was only one speed: full ahead.

All of them had a little blood on them. It was that intense. I don't know what they were playing for, but knowing Cal, it was probably just for pride. He was going after the puck-ball with the same energy he would go after a sharp grounder deep in the hole. Finally, Cal scored a goal past a diving Traber and the game ended and I shook hands with the future Hall of Famer and the rest of the Orioles make-shift hockey team.

That playfulness in Cal was a scene I saw many times during my tenure with the Orioles. I remember going down from the press box to the clubhouse during a rain delay at Memorial Stadium and in the back hallway leading to the clubhouse there was Cal, playing some kind of baseball game with the plastic top of a coffee can as the ball.

Then there was the night I was working late after a game and dropped into the spacious clubhouse at Camden Yards to leave some interview reminders for a couple of players for the next day. What I walked into — at 1:30 a.m. — was a full-fledged tape-ball game with Cal pitching against four or five of his teammates. This was after playing a 9-inning game.

What was going on in each of these scenarios? Fun.

Cal Ripken was as studious and as analytical as any player I have ever been around — but he never forgot to have fun. ☐

RICHARD VAUGHN SERVED AS PUBLIC RELATIONS DIRECTOR FOR THE ORIOLES FROM 1989 TO 1994. HE WAS ALSO THE TEAM'S DIREC-TOR OF MEDIA INFORMATION FROM 1985 TO 1988. HE IS CURRENT-LY THE VICE PRESIDENT OF PUBLIC RELATIONS FOR THE TAMPA BAY DEVIL RAYS.

– The Personal Side –

By | Bob Brown

Simply put, Cal Ripken Jr. was the best all-around shortstop in major league history.

Ripken's offensive contributions were immense and well catalogued both overall and exclusively as a shortstop. He was a two-time AL MVP, and a two-time All-Star Game MVP. He is one of only eight players to have recorded more than 400 home runs (431) and 3,000 hits (3,184). He established a new record for home runs by a shortstop with 345. He played 2,632 consecutive games to smash Lou Gehrig's 2,130 game mark. Included in that run were 2,216 straight games at shortstop, another major league record.

Ripken was the Orioles' third baseman at the start of the 1982 season (though he had played nine games at shortstop when he came up late in the previous season). He had primarily been a third baseman in the minors, but had appeared in 170 games at shortstop.

The move to shortstop was Manager Earl Weaver's idea, borne of necessity. Weaver had a problem at that time. He had three available shortstops on his 25-man roster (Kiko Garcia, Bob Bonner and Lenn Sakata), none of them likely to continue the Orioles tradition of excellence at the position (first there had been Luis Aparicio and then Mark Belanger).

It was then that Weaver made the brilliant, logical and generally unpopular move of shifting Ripken to short. He was too tall, his critics insisted. In fact, at 6-foot-4, he would become the tallest regular short-stop in baseball history. He was too big, they added, and he might have also been the heaviest although no one has proven that. And, he was also "too slow."

So, over the next 15 years or so (from July 1, 1982 through the 1996 season), Ripken went about proving his critics wrong.

· Ripken led AL shortstops in fielding percentage (twice), putouts (six times), assists (seven times), double plays (eight times), total chances (five times) and games played (12 times). He also won two Gold Gloves.

· Ripken set 11 AL or major league fielding records.

In 1990 he established a big league standard for highest fielding percentage (.996) after committing only three errors (a big league record) in 680 chances. He also played 95 consecutive errorless games (another record) and handled 431 consecutive errorless chances in that stretch (still another record). Note: Omar Visquel has since tied Ripken with 95 straight errorless games, and committing only three errors in 150 or more games in a season.

· Ripken also holds major league records for most double plays in a career at shortstop (1,565) and most assists in a season (583 in 1994).

During his consecutive-games streak, Ripken, like all hitters, slumped at the plate from time to time, which brought on the detractors again: "Get somebody in there who can hit." The only trouble was that the O's didn't have anybody who could play shortstop.

In other words, when Ripken wasn't hitting, he was still an asset defensively, and good defense has been a major factor in much of the Orioles' history.

What were the qualities that enabled Ripken to defy the physical profile that had dominated the position through the years? His legendary baseball instinct ("It's in the genes"), his superior intelligence, soft hands, a strong, accurate throwing arm, consistency, ability to concentrate under pressure, courage, durability and a love for the game that knows no bounds.

Among shortstops who have played 1,000 or more games, Ripken ranks fifth in lifetime fielding percentage (.97924). Vizquel, now with the Giants (.984), tops the list, followed ironically by Ripken's successor at short in Baltimore, Mike Bordick (.98056), the Phillies' Larry Bowa (.97986), and Toronto's Tony Fernandez (.97965). Just behind Ripken in sixth place is the Cardinals' legendary Hall of Famer, Ozzie Smith (.97863). Pretty good company.

By the way, Ripken was also able to extend the Orioles' tradition of excellence at shortstop, adding his name to those of Luis Aparicio and Mark Belanger. Subsequently, Bordick stretched that tradition still further. ☐

BOB BROWN SERVED AS DIRECTOR OF PUBLIC RELATIONS FOR THE ORIOLES FROM 1968 TO 1988. HE BEGAN WORKING FOR THE TEAM IN 1957 AND SPENT 35 YEARS WITH THE ORGANIZATION. HE IS CURRENTLY RETIRED.

www.kbank.net

K BANK

THE POWER OF K.

EQUAL OPPORTUNITY LENDER · Member FDIC

When we began to negotiate Cal Ripken Jr.'s 1992 contract, our company and the Orioles were a mere $30 million apart. Team officials wanted a four-year deal for $20 million and they cited, as their precedent, the salaries of the top shortstops in the game. We wanted a five-year contract and we cited, as our precedent and benchmark, the top players in the game, regardless of position. Our proposal approached $50 million.

Over the next 250 to 300 days, most of the negotiation concerned the money/time ratio. The Orioles slowly edged toward five years (fully justified by the trends in the game) and the dollars worked their way north of $25 million over the life of the contract. Our position moved down to the $35 million range. The key to coming

had clients and/or employers to represent.

How did we move from this phase to discovering each other's real interests? We changed locations from our offices, usually my conference room — jackets on, jackets off, sleeves rolled up, ties pulled down, crumpled yellow papers, cold coffee dregs in Styrofoam cups and a lineup of Diet Coke cans — and still little or no progress. We moved to my farm — outside, breeze blowing, overlooking a quiet pond, birds chirping in place of car horns. On the day in early summer when we sat at the farm, I thought another change might help: A deadline, not a threat, just a date we could all aim for. It was Cal's birthday, later in the summer, in August. It was far enough in the future that we both thought it was a good idea.

It was then that we started to hear each other, and we began to understand the other side's issues and interests.

THE ART OF THE DEAL

By | Ronald M. Shapiro

together was recognizing each other's interests.

Throughout the talks, the Orioles' negotiator was Larry Lucchino, a former tough trial lawyer turned baseball executive under former team owner Edward Bennett Williams and subsequent owner Eli Jacobs. Lucchino was one of the prime movers behind the creation of Camden Yards and today is part owner, president and CEO of the Boston Red Sox. He's a good friend but (unfortunately) he never let that stand in the way of saying "no" to me and the ballplayers I represented. Similarly, I didn't let our friendship get in the way of my asking for an aggressive, market-value contract for my client.

We were in the position phase — that is, I said, "This is why it's right for Cal Ripken to get at least $35 million" and he said, "This is why it's right that the Orioles only pay $25 million" — wherein both parties utter and repeat high-minded statements of belief and make very little practical movement. Our pronouncements were impassioned and sincere. Our verbal exchanges were heated and not always what you'd expect from friends. We each

Cal wanted a contract that acknowledged the totality of his accomplishments to date and took into account his contributions to community projects, his outside business ventures, and his future security. The team wanted a figure that acknowledged his recent decline in offensive statistics (though it was short-lived) and met the team's interests — fiscal responsibility, setting future contract precedents, yet still retaining one of the game's all-time greats. Lucchino was finally beginning to hear us. We were finally beginning to hear Lucchino and the Orioles.

We started to talk about ways to recognize Cal's contribution to the team in ways other than standard salary. For example, the Orioles eventually agreed to give Cal post-career compensation guarantees which added dollars to the overall contract but did not raise his pay for active years. (Interestingly, these very dollars were later traded for during-career compensation in his next contract.) They gave him merchandising rights in the stadium, another way to provide additional revenue for what Cal had come to represent but not pay for performance, per se. This

– The Art Of The Deal –

helped Cal provide funding for his recently created Kelly and Cal Ripken Jr. Charitable Foundation. The team offered special hotel accommodations on the road, designated parking, seats and a sky box for his family (which he paid for), all in an effort to provide added security as his increased visibility brought increased vulnerability.

Each of these creative solutions answered Cal's "interests." They provided the compensation he felt he had earned for his unflagging performance to the team and the town. At the same time, this form of reward

a top contract (albeit briefly) by getting a combination of revenue streams; and he got something else he truly wanted — to stay in the city he called home.

REPRINTED WITH PERMISSION FROM "THE POWER OF NICE: HOW TO NEGOTIATE SO EVERYONE WINS — ESPECIALLY YOU!" BY RONALD M. SHAPIRO AND MARK A. JANKOWSKI WITH JAMES DALE. PUBLISHED BY JOHN WILEY & SONS, INC. COPYRIGHT © 1998, 2001.

POSTSCRIPT On Aug. 24, 1992, the same day Cal Ripken signed his new contract with the Baltimore Orioles, Ron Shapiro was sitting in his usual seat — front row, down the third base line beside the visitors' dugout with an ice cream cone in his left hand and his 10-year-old son in his right. At that moment, former Orioles first baseman Randy Milligan laced a line drive foul ball that hooked dangerously into the seats. Amazingly, Ron caught the ball amid the cheers and praise of the fans for his unheralded bravery and focus.

The Orioles' tradition at the time followed that

allowed the club to maintain what it wanted, fiscal responsibility. The Orioles could keep his annual salary at a level they could live with.

On his birthday, Aug. 24, 1992, Cal signed the biggest contract of his career, 333 days after negotiations began. It was classic win-win. Both sides won. We felt Cal won a little more. The Orioles wanted a four-year deal. Cal wanted five years. Cal got his five. The Orioles didn't want to pay the highest salary of the day. They didn't. Cal would have been eligible for free agency a month and a half after the contract was signed. The bidding could have easily passed the $35 million mark, heading for $40 million. Instead, Cal got $32.5 million; he netted

when a fan caught an airborne foul ball, former public address announcer Rex Barney would tell the stadium to "Give that fan a contract!" Interestingly enough, when Ron caught Milligan's foul ball, Rex made no such statement. Later asked by then-*Baltimore Sun* reporter Ken Rosenthal why he refrained from addressing the fans with his patented statement, Rex jokingly responded, "He already had [a contract] and it was bigger and worth a whole lot more money than the one I can give him." □

ATTORNEY RONALD M. SHAPIRO SERVED AS CAL RIPKEN JR.'S AGENT DURING NEGOTIATIONS WITH THE ORIOLES. HE IS THE CO-FOUNDER AND CHAIRMAN OF THE SHAPIRO NEGOTIATIONS INSTITUTE.

DIETS DEMAND DAIRY DAILY

3-A-Day
Milk Cheese Yogurt
For stronger bones ®

The 2005 Dietary Guidelines for Americans sets up a foundation for healthy eating and recommends eating 3 servings of milk, cheese or yogurt each day for stronger bones and better bodies.

The Mid-Atlantic Dairy Association salutes
Cal Ripken Jr.

So you're about to go car shopping. Would it be helpful to know that Cal Ripken Jr. is a Chevy man? Or at least he says so in ads sprinkled all over the region. He's getting paid handsomely for the endorsement, but Chevy thinkers hope that will not matter a whole lot.

How about sneakers? Cal loves Nike. Same deal as Chevy, as well as for batteries (Energizer), satellite radio (XM), energy distributor (Constellation Energy) and telecommunications (Comcast). Plus, that cuddly ad with Cal on the ground with a couple of adorable girls is sure to get you to consider plucking Wisk laundry detergent off the shelf.

The Cal Commercial Crowd is large and devoted. He's more serious — and lucrative — as he approached and then broke Lou Gehrig's record for consecutive games played (2,130) on Sept. 6, 1995. Now that Cal has been elected into baseball's Hall of Fame, which amounts to sporting sainthood, you will see him even more frequently.

Cal's people are mum on exactly what ads will be peppering your consciousness leading up to and long after his induction into the Hall. But strategy was set a long time ago and, because they take lots of time to develop and shoot, the actual ads almost certainly have been in the can for weeks.

Perhaps not wanting anything to jinx his man, all the cautious Flannery would say during an interview prior to the Hall of Fame election was: "We anticipate a greater

MARKETING THE IRON MAN

By | Ken Denlinger

sneaky good in that regard. Q Rating measures popularity and, according to Chris Flannery, chief operating officer of Ripken Baseball, Ripken's popularity among sports figures is second only to Michael Jordan's. Behind Cal and in third place, Flannery said, is, ta da, Tiger Woods.

One of Cal's most devoted fans is Mamie Marlin, who lives by herself in the south-central Pennsylvania community of Peach Bottom. She's 91, and treasures an autographed picture of Cal.

"I remember the day Cal got married," Mamie said over the phone. "I remember the day his first child was born. I just love him: So honest, so good for everybody. I have his picture right in the living room, where I can sit and look at him."

Cal The Player began expanding into Cal The Pitchman early in his career, with Esskay some 23 years ago. His off-the-field business began to become

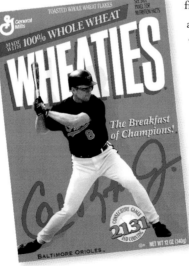

demand for his usage … He is a powerful figure who only enhances that (Hall of Fame) impact."

Nearly all the dozen or so endorsements (most fetching him in the mid to upper six figures each year) are long-term because, according to spokesman John Maroon, "it takes time to build momentum."

And those paying the tab seem more than satisfied.

"Price and affordability (in cars) drive everything, of course," said John Hammond, sales manager for Fitzgerald Auto Mall in Frederick. "But America's sports hero (Cal) and America's brand (Chevy) makes sense, goes hand in hand."

All this praise comes from a life-long Yankee fan.

"How can you not admire someone who showed up every day and gave 100 percent?" Hammond said.

Esskay folks are more effusive, possibly because the

– Marketing The Iron Man –

amount of money they paid Cal was right in the early-'80s and, to the amazement of many in sports marketing, has not changed all that much.

"Cal told his agents that since we were one of the first to give him an opportunity, that he would stay with us for as long as we wanted for about the same price," general manager Dave McLaughlin said. "Gotta like a guy like that. And he's exactly what he seems like (during his appearances for Esskay): professional, always prepared, and has a good time."

In nearly all of his endorsement contracts, Cal has the final say on when the appearances will be. And because Cal is aware of his responsibility to children, Maroon said, he will not be associated with beer or alcohol commercials, or have any tie-ins with gambling or casinos.

Maroon also said that Cal's perfectionist nature helps with ad preparation. He does not mind that a 30-second commercial might take eight hours to complete, that he might repeat the same 20-second line time after time after time until it's just right. He likes fussy directors.

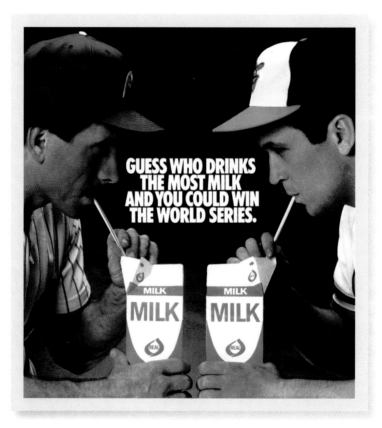

GUESS WHO DRINKS THE MOST MILK AND YOU COULD WIN THE WORLD SERIES.

One of the spots Cal surely enjoyed the most was one of the last ads he did for Coca-Cola, in 2001. Scheduled to shoot after a night game, the actual filming did not start until around 4 a.m., which made it as inconvenient as could be imagined. But Ripken was partnered with his daughter, Rachel.

Early on, according to his longtime agent Ron Shapiro, Ripken was conflicted when making a choice between two possible endorsements, the regional milk-marketing company or Jockey underwear. Actually, Cal could have done both. However, Shapiro said his advice to Cal

at that point in his career was fewer commercials — and Cal agreed.

Shapiro said Jockey wanted to use Cal as an addition to Oriole pitcher Jim Palmer, whose poses in underwear were rather daring for the times. Jockey paid more, nearly twice as much as the milk gig. Shapiro remembers asking Cal what may have been the pivotal question: Which would your mother prefer?

"Not to knock Jockey, but for what Cal sensed he stood for," Shapiro said, "milk made more sense."

In a seemingly seamless way, Cal has managed to bridge the gap between a celebrity and his public that so many athletes find impossible.

"It's not easy being him," Baltimore advertising executive Bob Leffler said. "And that's the whole point."

People trust him, which is the lynchpin of his endorsements.

Long ago, Cal joined Johnny Unitas and Brooks Robinson to form Baltimore's Holy Sports Trinity. (The Babe is by himself on another spiritual planet.) By leading the Colts to the 1958 NFL title, Unitas lifted Baltimore out of its mentality as a Triple-A city; Cal's pursuit of Gehrig's record raised civic self-esteem, coming as it did around the time the NFL turned down Baltimore as an expansion city.

It's probably pointless to argue who is No. 1, but Cal has an important leg up. Leffler explains: "Cal's a Marylander (Unitas was born in Pennsylvania, Robinson in Arkansas). That cements it all." □

KEN DENLINGER COVERED A VARIETY OF SPORTS FOR THE WASHINGTON POST FOR 38 YEARS.

SO THIS IS RETIREMENT?

By | Charlie Vascellaro

For a man known all of his life as "Junior" and largely defined by his relationship with his father, Cal Ripken Jr.'s life and career have come full circle. Since the end of his playing days, the man also known simply as "Cal" finds himself assuming a father figure's role, not only to his children, but to the youth baseball movement and baseball development industry as well.

It's a pretty big responsibility to live up to when the President of the United States shows up at your retirement party and says you're "the kind of man every father would like his son to be," as Bill Clinton did on Oct. 6, 2001.

Since hanging up his spikes, Ripken has made a smooth transition from ballplayer to businessman and baseball executive, stepping into his position as president and CEO of Ripken Baseball from the moment of his retirement as a player.

"It has been very enjoyable and very challenging," Ripken said. "In many ways I am a rookie in the business world and there is a lot to learn. That being said, I have found that there are many parallels between baseball and business and that has helped to make the transition smoother than expected. I have made it a point to meet as many successful people as I can and pick their brains. It has been a fun process."

The Ripken Baseball company, originally known as the Tufton Group, was established in 1991 to manage the numerous off-field opportunities Cal's iconic status and charisma brought his way. Ripken Baseball's mission/mantra is to grow the game of baseball worldwide "The Ripken Way," which is based on the coaching-teaching philosophy of Cal Ripken Sr. and stresses four points: Keep it Simple, Make it Fun, Explain Why and Celebrate the Individual (not over team; it just means that no two players are alike).

Brother Bill Ripken, who played with Cal in Baltimore during seven seasons, is his teammate once again as co-owner and executive vice president of Ripken Baseball and explains the family's life-calling.

"Everything that we have has come through baseball. We have a love for the game that was passed on to us through our dad. It seems a shame to waste such a passion," Bill Ripken said.

During his 21-year playing career Cal earned approximately $69 million in salary. By the time he was ready to retire, the foundation for the Ripken Baseball company was firmly in place in the form of four separate but related lucrative businesses that could earn Cal more money in his retirement than he made in his playing days.

Ripken Management and Design is a consulting company offering advice on baseball facilities design and management, field renovations and refurbishment as well as youth sports complex design and programs to municipalities, ownership groups and investors. It was created in 2001 and was the brainchild of Ripken's experience in getting his own minor league Aberdeen Ironbirds off the ground.

Cal purchased the Aberdeen Ironbirds in 2002. A New

"I HAVE FOUND THAT THERE ARE MANY PARALLELS BETWEEN BASEBALL AND BUSINESS."

– Cal Ripken Jr. –

– So This Is Retirement? –

York/Penn League Class-A affiliate of the Orioles based near Ripken's Havre de Grace birthplace, the team holds the distinction of being one of only two minor league franchises to sell out every home game of its first five seasons. Current Orioles, such as closer Chris Ray, outfielder Nick Markakis and pitcher Adam Loewen, are all Ironbirds alumni.

After four years of almost unparalleled success in running a minor league team, Ripken Baseball acquired another franchise in 2005, the Augusta Greenjackets. The Ripken Professional Baseball branch of the Ripken Baseball company has set a goal to acquire 10 more minor league clubs in the next 10 years.

The Ripkens began holding youth baseball camps and clinics in 1999, but the idea for the group of vintage major league replica fields like the ones at the Ripken Youth Baseball Academy in Aberdeen had its genesis on the night of Sept. 6, 1995. That's when the Major League Baseball Players Alumni Association, in honor of his breaking Lou Gehrig's consecutive-games streak, presented Cal with a check for $75,000 with which he could build his own "field of dreams." It was then Cal began to envision what would grow into his current complex.

And due to the success of the Aberdeen complex, Ripken Baseball opened another complex in Myrtle Beach, S.C., in June 2006. Like Aberdeen, the complex also houses youth baseball facilities with seven miniature replica major league ballparks from the past, including models of Old Comiskey Park, Ebbets Field and the Polo Grounds.

Aberdeen is also the permanent home of the Cal Ripken World Series, which is played each August and includes 15 teams of 11- and 12-year-olds from all over the world. In August the team from Hilo, Hawaii was crowned the champion of the 11-12-year-old bracket of the Cal Ripken Division.

Renamed from "Bambino" to "Cal Ripken" in 1999, the Ripken Division is the largest segment of Babe Ruth League Baseball with more than 700,000 participants covering ages 5-12.

Since 2003, the Ripken Baseball Complex has also served as host to a series of youth tournaments with a steady schedule running from March through November. In 2006 more than 800 teams comprised of 9-16-year-olds from 26 states participated in tournaments at the Aberdeen and Myrtle Beach facilities. In addition, more than 2,000 young players from 42 states and eight foreign countries attended camps and clinics on baseball and softball at the Ripken Academy.

The camp schedule runs from January through August, ranging from one-day clinics conducted at a cost of $140 to intense five-day overnight sessions with a $1,295 fee. Also, adults can attend the third-annual Ripken Minor League Experience fantasy camp and play ball with the Ripken brothers and other former Orioles. That program is scheduled for May 15-20, 2007 for $4,495.

– So This Is Retirement? –

A fifth business, Ironclad Authentics, a baseball memorabilia licensing company, was founded in 2004 with an online retail store where fans can purchase a Cal Ripken autographed baseball for $195 or a signed Miguel Tejada World Baseball Classic jersey for $395.

A visit to the Ripken Baseball website, www.ripkenbaseball.com, is a window into Cal's big world. It gives a tremendous amount of information about all of his and Bill's business interests and their entire corporate conglomeration, but let the web surfer beware: It can take hours to maneuver through.

Cal's post-retirement career actually began with the formation of The Cal Ripken Sr. Foundation, established in 2001. It is designed to teach life lessons through baseball to underprivileged youth across the country, as well as refurbishing sports fields throughout Maryland and making charitable donations in the form of baseball and softball equipment to school systems nationwide.

An important component of The Cal Ripken Sr. Foundation is also to educate young people on the dangers of using tobacco (Cal Sr. was a lifelong smoker who died of lung cancer).

Cal has also tried his hand as an author, collaborating again with brother Bill to write "Play Baseball the Ripken Way" in 2004 and "Parenting Young Athletes the Ripken Way" in 2006. He has also served as a weekly advice columnist for the *Baltimore Sun* since October 2005.

Commercial endorsements have also been a large part of Cal's post-playing career. He's been a regular fixture on billboards, television and radio, hawking for companies like XM, Chevy, Comcast, Nike, Wisk, Energizer and DHL.

Many have speculated about Cal's coaching or managing in the minors or big leagues some day.

"Coaching is something that has always been of interest to me and I get some of that when I teach the kids at our camps," Ripken said. "If I were to get back into Major League Baseball, my interest would be to impact an entire organization and help shape it from the ground up. As I have said many times, if that opportunity were to one day present itself, I would be smart enough to listen."

It has been a foregone conclusion since the day he retired, but now it is official that Cal will be inducted into Cooperstown. In the meantime, Cal has remained humble about his impending honor.

"I have made a real effort to put it out of my mind. If it does happen it will be one of the great honors of my life," Ribken said. "I was lucky enough to be at Eddie Murray's induction and it was extremely powerful and emotional." ☐

CHARLIE VASCELLARO IS A WRITER WHO SPECIALIZES IN BASEBALL AND BASEBALL HISTORY AND THE AUTHOR OF A BIOGRAPHY OF HANK AARON.

ALL IN THE CARDS

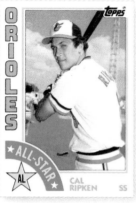

1984

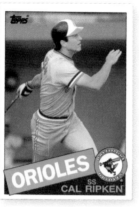

1985

1986

1987

1988

1989

1990

1991

1992

1993

1994

1995

1996   1997   1998   1999

THE ORIOLES FUTURE STARS

BOBBY BONNER

- FULL NAME: Robert Averill Bonner
- HEIGHT: 6' 0"   WEIGHT: 185
- BATS: Right   THROWS: Right
- BORN: August 12, 1956 (Uvalde, Texas)
- Drafted by the Orioles in the third round of the 1978 draft (74th overall selection), Bonner played 61 games for the Orioles from 1980 to 1983.

BOB BONNER Shortstop   **CAL RIPKEN** 3rd Base   **JEFF SCHNEIDER** Pitcher

Topps BALTIMORE ORIOLES FUTURE STARS

Cal Ripken Jr. was one of three players featured on a Topps 1982 Baltimore Orioles Future Stars card.

The other two? Shortstop Bob Bonner and pitcher Jeff Schneider. We all know how the "future" panned out for Ripken. Whatever happened to Bonner and Schneider?

JEFF SCHNEIDER

- FULL NAME: Jeffrey Theodore Schneider
- HEIGHT: 6' 3"   WEIGHT: 195
- THROWS: Left
- BORN: December 6, 1952 (Bremerton, Wash.)
- Drafted by the Orioles from the Philadelphia Phillies in the 1978 Rule V Draft, Schneider pitched in 11 games for the Orioles in 1981. Schneider was traded by the Orioles to the Angels in the winter of 1982 in a deal which sent Schneider and Doug DeCinces to California for outfielder Dan Ford.

– BOBBY BONNER –

Year	Team	G	AB	R	H	2B	3B	HR	RBI	BB	SO	SB	OBP	SLG	AVG
1980	BAL	4	4	1	0	0	0	0	1	0	0	0	.000	.000	.000
1981	BAL	10	27	6	8	2	0	0	2	1	4	1	.310	.370	.296
1982	BAL	41	77	8	13	3	1	0	5	3	12	0	.198	.234	.169
1983	BAL	6	0	0	0	0	0	0	0	0	0	0	.000	.000	.000
Totals:		61	108	15	21	5	1	0	8	4	16	1	.219	.259	.194

– JEFF SCHNEIDER –

Year	Team	W	L	ERA	G	GS	CG	SHO	SV	IP	H	R	ER	HR	HBP	BB	SO
1981	BAL	0	0	4.88	11	0	0	0	1	24	27	15	13	4	1	12	17

PressBox | On Sept. 20, 1998, you had played and started in 2,632 consecutive games. You walked into Ray Miller's office about 30 minutes before game time, and asked him to take you out of the lineup. How long had you contemplated that, and why that night?

Cal Ripken | It was a spur-of-the-moment decision. I had thought about it early in the year ... I can't remember what exactly made me think of it, but I just thought that the time was right. I said, "Well, if we fall out of the race, then it would be a good time to put an end to it."

... I talked to Kelly, my wife, and she said, "You can't do it the last day of the season, it's in Boston. Everybody's followed your career, they've loved what you've done, it's been for all the right reasons, it's been positive. You

the bench, let me take an occasional half-inning inside the clubhouse and see what happens in there," because these things I never knew about. I was always in the game and I didn't know what everyone else was doing. I chose to experience things in different ways during that game. It did turn out to truly be a celebration, turned out to be the right way to put it to bed.

PB | After having started that many consecutive games, how difficult were those last three seasons, 1999-2001, when due to the back injuries and the aging process, you were more limited in your ability to play and how you could perform?

CR | You need to rely on a healthy structure, and I was anything but that. The game's hard enough as it is, without

Q&A WITH BASEBALL'S IRON MAN

should do it during the last game at home, if that's what you decide to do."

I thought about it, and she made a lot of sense. It just happened that it was the Yankees on the last home game of the season. When I came in, there was a sense of anticipation, I guess, because I was probably the only one who knew, besides my wife and very few people within our inner circle that I had confided in. I went into Ray Miller's office. It was a total surprise to him. I wanted to do it late enough, where I wouldn't have to deal with it before the game started.

The funny part was that Ryan Minor didn't want to take the field, and I had to convince him that it wasn't a rookie prank; he should go out on the field. I almost had to push him out onto the field. Then, it was a celebration of just enjoying the game and saying goodbye to The Streak. My goal was, "Let me go out in the bullpen and see what these bullpen guys do. Let me sit on

having to deal with injuries. It gave me a great perspective on some of the guys that haven't been as lucky as me to not be injured and to play with those sorts of things for their whole careers.

I became a little more understanding of people who couldn't play the 162-game schedule, for whatever reason ... I remember fans saying, "I drove all the way to come see you, and you didn't even play." That was something that everyone took for granted, for all those years, no matter when they came to see the Orioles play, they could always count on the fact that I was going to be in there. It's something that didn't really resonate with me, I knew I was going to be in there, and I knew all the right reasons of wanting to play, but I never heard it from the fans' perspective before. It almost made me feel bad, that I didn't live up to the expectation, that I wasn't in the lineup, but it also made me feel good. For all those years, you could count on me.

– Q&A With Baseball's Iron Man –

PB | During the '99 season you had to deal with the loss of your father, injuries and you got your first glimpse of what life could be without baseball. Was that a key season in transitioning to what you've become in your post-playing career?

CR | Being on the disabled list gave me a chance to catch my breath, grieve a little bit, and then look at life in the perspective that it wasn't all about baseball, that there was a bigger meaning in life that included baseball. During the course of that summer, it was one of the more enjoyable summers as a hitter, I was hitting about .340 in September. I felt like my body was okay, it was acting pretty well, but there was some question whether I was going to have surgery or not. But at the time I was thinking, "Well, if this continues up, I won't need to have surgery." I needed to have some sort of indication of what I should do. Sure enough, I think it was Sept. 21, I hit a base hit to right field, and I slipped a little bit, and felt something give in my back. I didn't think it was much, but the next day, the same sort of pain came through my leg. Then, I was on a plane heading to Cleveland to get the procedure done.

I think the question was, "Did your perspective change?" You know, I enjoyed that season, baseball-wise, as much as any season. It seemed like Dad was watching over me. Things came easy offensively, and I felt like my old self, in many ways, and then surgery kind of snaps you back into it.

From that point on, with the surgery, it became a struggle. I was limited. I was on a rehab offseason, and then the next year was a struggle, trying to get my body back. Ironically, it wasn't until my last offseason that I felt that I had my body back underneath me. I probably was in better shape going in, right before I broke my rib, going into that spring training than I had been for four or five years. I was going to lay it all on the line and see where it ended up. I broke my rib about a week before spring training, and that put me behind the eight-ball.

The last three or four years were a struggle physically. It also gave me a view into my next life, my next career, what that could be. Fortunately, I was young enough and my kids were young enough where I could enjoy that part of my life, whereas my dad didn't get a chance to enjoy that with us as much. I felt there was something more and something else waiting for me beyond baseball. It doesn't mean I cared less about baseball; I was ready physically and emotionally to move on.

PB | Jim Palmer always says, "The thing I miss most was the camaraderie with teammates, when I left the game." What did you miss most about the game?

CR | Well, I'm at a position now where I can understand that. I think we as people, we want to belong to something. Baseball players spend their whole life belonging to a team, and then all of a sudden you're not on a team anymore. So now, I can fully understand what that means. Although, in many ways, starting these businesses, I create a different sort of team. So I can hold on to those people experiences, plus I still play basketball and have people over. I can get the artificial feeling of a team in the locker room as I had all those years at my house. Athletes spend their whole life working and belonging to something, and then there's a transition period afterward. I don't know if mine was smoother than some. I know that I had plans and knew what I wanted to do, and maybe on my terms,

– Q&A With Baseball's Iron Man –

it made the transition a little easier. But even then, when you look at baseball from the front-row seats, behind the stands, you still look at it from the outside looking in. For all those years, I looked at it from the inside looking out.

PB | A lot of people say that your streak saved baseball, after what happened in 1994 with the strike and the loss of the World Series. How does Cal Ripken see that?

CR | (Chuckles) I think it's a stretch. It's very complimentary, and if I played a small role in it, then I feel happy that I could do that. I think it was a matter of timing. I think after '94 and the cancellation of the World Series, everybody wanted something to hold onto that was good. I think the streak became that link to a past time when people thought about the game differently. So as the streak went on, I guess the concept of surrendering to it, kind of going with the flow as opposed to fighting it, and not letting it impact my day-to-day activities...surrendering to it made it easier with the fans, easier with the media, easier with my teammates. I think it truly was just a matter of timing; that people started to relate to that, and they were looking for something good in baseball, and I became a part of that.

PB | What do you think makes somebody worthy of the Hall of Fame?

CR | I think that's almost indefinable. It was a dream experience as a kid, wanting to be a baseball player, wanting to get to the big leagues. Once you get to the big leagues, you want to have a good career and stay. I don't think it's in your mind that you'll be worthy enough for the Hall of Fame. The Hall of Fame is a celebration of the game's best players. It's a celebration of the history of baseball. We all in our minds want to leave our mark in some ways, that we made a contribution to make the game better. I

"WE ALL IN
OUR MINDS
WANT TO LEAVE
OUR MARK
IN SOME WAYS."

– CAL RIPKEN JR. –

guess leaving your mark in a big enough way celebrates you in the Hall of Fame, but I don't know how to define it. That's certainly not a statistical achievement, solely. It's very subjective in many ways, because after all, human beings are voting for it. So, I don't know. I never really gave it much thought to who's deserving and who's not.

PB | You saw The Oriole Way from childhood until it was sort of extinguished due to the changes in the game with money and free agency, some mismanagement, and things of that nature. In 1983, given what the Orioles had meant to baseball the preceding 25 years, if I had said, "That's it, it's going to be 23 years and they won't have competed in a World Series again," what would you have said then?

CR | I would have said, "You're out of your mind." (Chuckles) I thought that in my first two years, that this was the way it was going to be every year, going to the last day of the season... I still think the most exciting series I've ever played in was the four games against Milwaukee, having won the doubleheader, and winning the Saturday game, I think the Sunday game was the deciding one ... and then taking that experience and applying it to the next year and taking it a little further and winning the World Series, I thought, "This is Orioles baseball, this is Orioles history." Then in a short period of time, having gone through a rebuilding process, and then being the only one left from that '83 team. When I think of people like Derek Jeter, I guess they don't know how good they've got it. Every year, a bad year for them is losing in the first round of the playoffs, as opposed to going through rebuilding processes. The Orioles organization changed, a lot of the key players changed, a lot of the key people that were considered part of The Oriole Way moved on.

The Orioles were the model organization, where not

– Q&A With Baseball's Iron Man –

only did it produce players for the rest of the league, it seemed like when you needed a manager, you came into that staff and took a manager. I guess that's the normal process with success, you can't hang on to all of your good people, and a lot of change occurred. As I said before, I was the only one left from the '83 championship team in a hurry. Then you deal with the different rebuilding situations and try to do what you can with the process. I certainly would've liked to be on the winning end more often than I was. It was satisfying to get back to the playoffs in '96 and '97, to reestablish a sense of pride, to go into Yankee Stadium and have a real meaningful series, the way it used to be, and to prevail and win.

I guess in some cases, you don't really learn the lesson until you feel both sides of it. You really can't appreciate winning as much unless you've endured the frustrations of losing. To finally get back, it was worth the struggle.

PB Brooks Robinson was your idol; and also Mark Belanger was, I guess, somewhat of a mentor to you early on...

CR Yeah, Belanger was a great teacher. I don't know if people understand that. He was technical in his angles, and in his understanding of the position. He was a student of the game at shortstop. I don't know too many people that really understood shortstop the way he did. When I was 14, he was telling me things about going into the hole, and backhanding off of your throwing leg, or taking this angle to the ball. I couldn't understand it, but I listened to the words, and as I played the game, then there were times when I understood what he was talking about. When I came to the

big leagues in '81, he was still there. I got called up in August, and I played in the first couple of games. Then, in the month of September, I was pretty much sitting on the bench watching. So I sat with Mark Belanger, and he would point out things that other shortstops were doing. He said, "Look, when you're on the bench over here, you don't just think about hitting. Watch the other guy out there on defense. Not too many people understand thinking about defense when you're on the bench, but you should do both."

As I became more of a thinker at the position, it was right up my alley, because I like to understand why, how, different ways to do things, and he was perfect for that. I don't know if he was a mentor, but he certainly was a great teacher...

Brooksie was a teacher by example; Belanger was a teacher by words and by example. All of us could watch Brooksie and figure out how to make that barehanded play on the run, but Belanger was so fundamental and his angles were so good that he had the appearance that he wasn't doing anything flashy, which turned out to be my trademark.

PB Your performance at the beginning of your career is almost unbelievable. Was that just physical maturity, was it learning the game?

CR It was learning yourself, it was learning how to wait on the ball. Your power is a combination of your timing and the speed of the bat. A lot of young players, including myself, you lose a lot of your power by starting the bat too soon. Once you learn to wait a little bit longer and explode all at once, then you start to understand your power.

– Q&A With Baseball's Iron Man –

PB | How would you classify yourself as a hitter?

CR | Home run leaders led the league in home runs with 37. I thought anybody that could hit 20 home runs a year was considered someone with home run power. I had gap power, where I could hit doubles and drive the ball into the gap, but also had the ability to hit the ball over the fence. I was a line drive hitter, more of a ground-ball, line drive hitter. My home runs weren't towering home runs; they were line drives that carried over the fence.

PB | How would you define your career as a player? You had 400 home runs, you had 3,000 hits, and you had the streak. Some people have said, "Well, if it wasn't for the streak, he wouldn't go into the Hall of Fame."

CR | I don't look at myself that way. The streak was not born out of me deciding early on that I wanted to be a record holder in the streak. It was managers like Earl and Joe and Frank who wrote my name in the lineup. I had no power over those guys. It was my desire to come to the ballpark and play every day. That totally was from Dad's approach. Dad's approach to being a professional baseball player was to come to the ballpark ready to play. I think one of the compliments, and this is how people ask me all the time, "How would you like to be remembered?" There's an expression, "being a gamer." You come to the ballpark, waiting to meet the challenges of the day and trying to help your team win. Is it easy? No. Is it easier to take a day off if you're struggling and Roger Clemens happened to be pitching that next day? Probably, but it's not your job to determine that. Your job is to try to do the best that you can every day.

PB | Now that it's here, what does it feel like, knowing you're going to go into the Hall of Fame, knowing that this is going to happen?

> ℞
>
> "YOU REALLY CAN'T APPRECIATE WINNING AS MUCH UNLESS YOU'VE ENDURED THE FRUSTRATIONS OF LOSING."
>
> – CAL RIPKEN JR. –

CR | You know me; I try hard not to get ahead of myself. I try hard to keep perspective and cope with things. It doesn't do you any good to start to play out "What if?" Those things help when you're standing at shortstop, thinking, "OK, if the ground ball's hit to me, what do I do with it?" How you're going to be looked upon when you've finished your career, I remember a lot of people asked those questions, and I used to always say, "When I'm in that position, sitting in my rocking chair, maybe I'll have a different perspective, but now, you've got to play."

If I was asked the question beforehand, I really don't have an answer. The only thing I can do is react to it and prepare for it if it does happen.

PB | How seriously do you take your new position with kids' sports, almost being anointed as a spokesperson for what can and should be right with youth sports?

CR | I try to maintain perspective in all areas, because I think I get too much credit. I get too much attention for some of the things that I've been able to accomplish. Baseball's a great game; Dad instilled a love of baseball into me from a very early age, just by his love and what he did. He made a nice contribution to the game, and I went on to make a nice contribution to the game. I feel very strongly about trying to pass on that experience, that love of the game to as many people as I can. When someone refers to me as the "ambassador of baseball," I kind of laugh internally, and I think that they're complimentary things to say, but I feel good in the fact that you're being recognized for doing some good things in baseball. I think the important thing is to impact kids in a positive way, so they can go on and have a good, full life. ☐

THIS INTERVIEW WAS CONDUCTED BY STAN "THE FAN" CHARLES AND JIM HENNEMAN IN NOVEMBER 2006.

al Ripken Jr. has been credited with leaving a great impact on Major League Baseball. Many believe that as a successful 6-foot-4 shortstop, he changed the perception that shortstops had to be of small stature, paving the way for players such as Derek Jeter, Alex Rodriguez and Nomar Garciaparra to be given the opportunity to play the position.

In 1991 Ripken became the first American League player (and the third player in history) to win the Most Valuable Player award while playing for a losing team (Alex Rodriguez has since won the award while playing for a losing team). This reopened debate regarding the definition of an MVP.

But perhaps the strongest impact — and hardest to

many disillusioned fans back.

One of the things that sets baseball apart from other major sports is the regard for the records and history that are associated with it. Of all of the hallowed records and statistics that are quoted on a daily basis by fans everywhere (Cy Young's 511 wins, Hank Aaron's 755 home runs, Pete Rose's 4,256 hits), there was only one that was thought to be unbreakable.

Lou Gehrig was one of the game's greatest players. Of all the Hall of Fame numbers he put up in his career, it is his durability for which he is best remembered. From 1925 to 1939, Gehrig played in an incredible 2,130 consecutive games. Gehrig eventually succumbed to a fatal illness that ended the streak. His consecutive-games string of 2,130 games was called the record that could

RIPKEN TO THE RESCUE

By | Allen V. McCallum Jr.

prove — that Ripken had on the game came in 1995. That season, Cal Ripken Jr. saved the game of baseball.

On Aug. 12, 1994 the Major League Baseball Players Association began a strike that lasted for 234 days and eliminated the 1994 World Series. Baseball became the first major sport to fail to have a postseason due to a labor conflict; there was no World Series champion for the first time in 90 years.

The strike continued into the following spring. The 1995 season began on April 25. By that time, much damage had been done. Many baseball fans were disillusioned by the actions of both players and owners. While unions going on strike to demand better working conditions and wages is a time-honored labor strategy in America, it was very difficult for the public to identify with millionaires going to war against billionaires. There was little public sympathy for either side during the strike.

After the initial shock subsided, fans found other things to do during the late summer and fall months, and they simply gravitated away from baseball. It took the breaking of a major record and the subsequent spotlight on one of the game's favorite sons to bring

never be broken, but, as the strike came to an end in April 1995, buzz started to build for a feat that would put an end to that saying.

Ripken had played in every game for the Baltimore Orioles since his rookie year in 1982. Playing at one of the most demanding positions on the field, Ripken's durability became legendary over the next 13 seasons. While Gehrig was known to only play one inning or so on occasion to keep his streak alive, Ripken's streak included nothing so artificial. From June 5, 1982 to Sept. 14, 1987, Cal played 8,243 consecutive innings, a number believed to be the major league record. (MLB does not keep official records of consecutive innings played.) The consecutive-innings streak spanned 904 games. Through the length of his consecutive-game streak, Ripken played in 99.8 percent of the innings in which the Orioles participated.

During Ripken's consecutive-game streak, he won the Rookie of the Year award in 1982, two MVPs (1983, 1991), two Gold Gloves (1991, 1992) and a world championship in 1983. Ripken put up the bulk of the numbers that made him one of only eight players in the history of the game to have the combination of 3,000 hits and 400

– Ripken To The Rescue –

home runs, and the only full-time infielder to do so.

Ripken played through swollen ankles, twisted knees, profound offensive slumps and the birth of a child. (Ryan Ripken, Cal and Kelly Ripken's second child, was born on an off day for the Orioles.) Despite injury and distraction, Ripken played on.

Ripken played several seasons in which his offensive production declined, and in those times the streak was often called into question. Many critics said Ripken should sit down for the good of the team. To some the streak was seen as a selfish record that was hurting his club, and his reputation.

One of the great ironies of Ripken's career was that in many of the seasons when his offensive production was down, he played his best defense. In 1990, he had one of his poorest offensive seasons. In June of that year, Ripken saw his batting average in the low-.200s. While finishing the season at .250, his power and production numbers were his worst to that point in his career.

During the same season, Ripken carried another consecutive streak. He went 95 straight games without an error (a record at that time), and finished the season with only three errors and a .996 fielding percentage (also a major league record). There is no question that the consecutive-games streak was filled with controversy over the years for Ripken. However, in 1995, the timing for Ripken and his streak proved to be perfect for a damaged sport.

Ripken was a fan favorite in many cities. In fact, it was only in Baltimore that his legacy as a player would be debated. In most cities, Ripken was viewed as the best kind of player. He was a throwback, a player reminiscent of bygone days. He played every day. He played in one uniform, for one team, during his entire career. Ripken was viewed as one of the most hard-nosed players of his generation.

As the season prepared for its late start during 1995,

the possibility of Ripken breaking Gehrig's hallowed record was noteworthy. Ripken appeared on the cover of industry periodicals repeatedly throughout the 1995 season. He sat through countless interviews as well. It was as if the media was trying to latch on to the one positive in the game for the fans.

Ripken would do his part beyond the view of the cameras as well. Even before '95, Ripken was known for his prolific signing of autographs. In 1995, he turned it up by several notches. Ripken was seen signing autographs for hours after games. At home or on the road, he was there. The line of autograph seekers, young and old, would span for rows just above the dugout, and Ripken was at the end of it, signing for as long as two or three hours after games.

At a time when fans had every right to boo baseball players everywhere, or take them to task for the callous nature of the business end of the game, Ripken and his much-debated streak proved to be a solitary lightning rod for pulling the focus back onto the field, and illustrating what was good about the game.

As Sept. 6 approached, the sports talk shows and media outlets began discussing what was important about the streak. There was no single moment to focus on. When Hank Aaron broke Babe Ruth's all-time home run record, there was the blast from his mighty bat over the left-center field wall in Atlanta-Fulton County Stadium. After days of anticipation, the moment caused an eruption from his fans, teammates and the broadcasters who called the game. When Pete Rose broke Ty Cobb's all-time hits record, the focus was the solid opposite-field line drive into left-center field in Cincinnati. The salute the home fans offered him brought tears to Rose's eyes as he stood at first base.

Critics argued that there was no singular moment, no talisman to celebrate as Ripken simply "played another game." The Orioles came up with a way to remedy that.

– Ripken To The Rescue –

In the second half of the '95 season during the fifth inning of all Oriole home games, the Jumbotron showed the MLB definition of an official game. With John Tesh's "Day One" playing in the background, numbers placed on the Camden Yards warehouse would drop to mark the addition of one more game in the streak.

This became the singular moment that people waited for each night. Initially, people thought it was a goofy idea that took too much time. As the record-breaking game drew closer, however, people began to appreciate the moment. Like a pendulum swinging on a grandfather clock, it crystallized the passing of time, and the magnitude of Ripken's accomplishment.

While baseball is a game that is played without a clock, it pays more tribute to the passing of time than any other. Those numbers on the warehouse seemed to reach back to Ripken's rookie season, and a time when he said that he just hoped to be able to play every day. They reached back to the months before the strike when what happened on the field was the topic of conversation. They seemed to reach back to Gehrig and the days when the Iron Horse became a legend in New York and in the baseball world.

The entire sports world descended on Camden Yards on the nights of Sept. 5 and 6, 1995. Everything about those nights seemed perfectly planned. From "The Star-Spangled Banner" performed by Bruce Hornsby and Branford Marsalis, to the dropping of the numbers, to Ripken hitting home runs in three consecutive games, the excitement of those nights grew into the culmination of the 22-minute trip around the ballpark when Cal shook hands and accepted congratulations from everyone close enough to get to him.

The energy in the ballpark that night would go out beyond the park itself. Throughout the country, you could feel baseball fans thanking Ripken for giving them something positive to look forward to during the entire '95 season. It was truly the right record at the right time.

While some were of the opinion that a man showing up for work every day was no big deal, to others the streak

symbolized a commitment to the game that was missing during the strike. While free agents changed teams, and players would sit out of games for the smallest of injuries, and people who would never have to worry about money fought over that very item, Cal Ripken played for one team every day, and virtually every inning of every game.

The game has survived many tumultuous moments. From the Chicago Black Sox, to the creation of the players union, to the collusion of the late-'80s, the game has had to find ways to weather the storm. There is always a Babe Ruth, or a Reggie Jackson, or a polarizing moment that fans can latch onto and bring them back to the game. The game would not have died if Ripken's record had not come along. There would have been another moment, or another record, perhaps farther down the road.

In 1998 Mark McGwire and Sammy Sosa battled the entire season to break Roger Maris' single-season home run record. Each did it, but McGwire finished by wearing the crown with 70 home runs struck. Many pointed to this season as the season that sent baseball back into prominence.

The difference is that Ripken's moment was simple and pure. In the years following '98, the Ruthian feats of McGwire and Sosa have been called into question due to the revelations concerning performance-enhancing substances running rampant in the game. Nothing so artificial can taint what Cal Ripken Jr. did for baseball. His contribution was about honoring the game by giving it all that you have, and leaving it all on the field.

Whether he did or did not save the game, there can be no question that Ripken gave it the jump-start it dearly needed in one of its darkest hours. In years to come, when people visit the Hall of Fame in Cooperstown and see the plaque that carries Ripken's likeness, someone will ask if he really saved baseball. There is a pretty good chance that the reply to that question will be, "Yes." ☐

IT WAS TRULY THE RIGHT RECORD AT THE RIGHT TIME.

ALLEN V. MCCALLUM JR. IS A BASEBALL ANALYST FOR WNST RADIO AND A CONTRIBUTING COLUMNIST FOR PRESSBOX.

Today we consider Cal Ripken Jr. the luckiest man on the face of the earth.

Eleven years after he passed the ghost of Lou Gehrig and assured his ticket to Cooperstown, Ripken heads to baseball's Hall of Fame as the embodiment of the American Dream.

He played major league baseball in the shadow of his hometown. He followed his daddy to spring training every year and tagged along behind big kids named Robinson and Palmer and Powell. When he arrived at Memorial Stadium to start hitting home runs, it was proud Cal Sr. extending his hand from the third base coach's box, and then it was brother Bill taking the second base flip to start a double play. If that's not the stuff of every kid's wiffle ball dreams, then what is?

born, sit down for the good of the club and stop thinking about records.

Cal insisted the streak had nothing to do with it, he was just trying to put in an honest day's work. Sometimes his stubbornness seemed maddening. But then, knowing Cal as we did, we understood that it was such stubbornness that helped make him so indomitable an athlete. So even the doubters among us applauded what seemed like a throwback work ethic, a desire to earn his paycheck.

When Cal finally took a breather, the streak had reached 2,632 games. When he finally sat down for good, he was one of just seven players in history with both 3,000 hits and 400 home runs, and he had protected the left side of the Orioles infield immaculately across two decades.

OUR HOMETOWN HERO

By | Michael Olesker

On the night he erased Gehrig's consecutive-game record, Cal kissed his wife and kids behind home plate, and waved to his parents, and then triumphantly circled the field for fans who embraced him as a surrogate brother or son.

Cal was that nice neighborhood boy we had watched grow into a fine young man. When he retired five years ago, his image was so wholesome that he collected money every time he held up a glass of milk in public.

He was the carrier of fantasies ingrained in the souls of generations of American youngsters: extending the neighborhood pitch-and-catch as far as it could take him. He was the ordinary working stiff who made himself immortal by showing up at the job every day when it would have been much easier to take an occasional breather.

And, as the inevitable Iron Horse comparisons were made, he was humble enough to admit he was not Lou Gehrig, he was only Cal Ripken. Gehrig hit .340 over his abbreviated lifetime, and Ripken hit .276. Even in his fulsome years, there were five seasons when Cal's average did not reach .260, and more than a few nights when the radio talk show voices insisted he stop being so stub-

Consider a few more numbers, even more remarkable: Over the course of the streak, 3,711 injured major league players were placed on the disabled list. That computes, over 13 seasons, to 285 players per year. There are 25 players on a major league team. Thus, the equivalent of nearly 12 full teams per year landed on the list — while Cal played on with fastballs buzzing past his head and runners in spikes nipping at his ankles.

On the night Ripken tied Gehrig's record, he hit a home run. On the night he broke the record, he hit another. When the fifth inning passed and the record was officially his, he doffed his cap shyly to wave to the roaring crowd. And we noticed, not for the first time, the changes that time had wrought. The boy who had sprouted in our midst had become a man with a graying, almost bare pate. It was our gentle reminder: We'd spent all those years growing older together.

When he took his lap around the ballpark that night, and all those hands reached out to grasp his for a moment, it wasn't just Cal we were watching but a kaleidoscope of memories that stretched from 33rd Street down to South

– Our Hometown Hero –

Baltimore, from the briefly triumphant Ripken-Eddie Murray era to the wilderness years when Cal seemed the last carrier of a vanishing culture.

He had arrived just in time for the Orioles' last great hurrah. In his Rookie of the Year season, 1982, the Orioles were still affectionately known as The Best Team Money Can't Buy. They almost pulled off a stretch-drive miracle before losing on the final day of the season. They were world champs the next year, when Ripken was the Most Valuable Player and squeezed that final line drive to clinch the World Series victory over Philadelphia.

But two decades later Ripken departed in the midst of an endless Sahara of losing seasons. The team that had won two world championships, five pennants and five division titles before he arrived would never again in Ripken's time reach the World Series after 1983.

In the absence of team success, Cal became a focal point of our affection. We loved him for staying through good times and bad. Even in the Orioles' brief run of excellence in the '90s, there was something special about Ripken. He was no longer the best player on the team. But he was ours.

We marveled at Roberto Alomar's magic, and at Rafael Palmeiro's sweet swing. But they were just guys passing through, and made no secret of it. They were highly paid itinerant laborers. They had no investment in Baltimore, and so we barely had time to invest any emotions in them. They weren't our kids. They weren't Ripken, who grew up in the neighborhood, or Brooksie or Palmer or Murray, who came up through the home team system.

So even when we had our frustrations with him, we loved Cal for being the last of a breed, the final remnant of a system called The Oriole Way. He was our reminder that we had once imagined it would always be that way: familiar Oriole faces, consistent Oriole triumphs.

Baseball is our great maker of myth. We want to believe our heroes represent not only our team, but our town. We want to believe our love for them is requited. It's why we held Cal so close to our hearts, even in the worst of summers. We knew his history, and his whole family's. We'd watched him play out the story that could have been our own. He was our closest connection to the great American Dream. In Cal, we could actually reach out and touch it. ☐

MICHAEL OLESKER IS CURRENTLY A COLUMNIST FOR THE BALTIMORE EXAMINER.

BY THE NUMBERS

2,632 Consecutive games played by Cal Ripken Jr., beginning on May 30, 1982 and ending on Sept. 20, 1998

8,243 Consecutive innings played by Cal Ripken Jr., spanning 904 games before ending on Sept. 14, 1987

11,551 Career at bats for Cal Ripken Jr.

3,184 Career hits for Cal Ripken Jr.

431 Career home runs for Cal Ripken Jr.

8 Players in Major League Baseball history with 400+ home runs and 3,000+ hits:
Hank Aaron (755 / 3,771) · Willie Mays (660 / 3,283)
Rafael Palmeiro (569 / 3,020) · Eddie Murray (504 / 3,255)
Stan Musial (475 / 3,630) · Dave Winfield (465 / 3,110)
Carl Yastrzemski (452 / 3,419) · Cal Ripken Jr. (431/ 3,184)

7 Numbers retired by the Orioles, including Cal Ripken Jr.'s No. 8, which was retired by the Orioles before the final home game of the 2001 season:
4 - Earl Weaver · 5 - Brooks Robinson
8 - Cal Ripken Jr. · 20 - Frank Robinson
22 - Jim Palmer · 33 - Eddie Murray
42 - Jackie Robinson (RETIRED BY ALL MLB TEAMS IN 1997)